Preaching the Gospel to Yourself

HOW THE GOSPEL TRANSFORMS
EVERYDAY LIFE

JOANNA KIMBREL & STEFANIE BOYLES

Study Suggestions

Thank you for choosing this study to help you dig into God's Word.
We are so passionate about women getting into Scripture, and we are
praying that this study will be a tool to help you do that.

————————

Here are a few tips to help you get the most from this study:

- Before you begin, take time to look into the context of the book. Find out who wrote it and learn about the cultural climate it was written in, as well as where it fits on the biblical timeline. Then take time to read through the entire book of the Bible we are studying if you are able. This will help you to get the big picture of the book and will aid in comprehension, interpretation, and application.

- Start your study time with prayer. Ask God to help you understand what you are reading and allow it to transform you (Psalm 119:18).

- Look into the context of the book as well as the specific passage.

- Before reading what is written in the study, read the assigned passage! Repetitive reading is one of the best ways to study God's Word. Read it several times, if you are able, before going on to the study. Read in several translations if you find it helpful.

- As you read the text, mark down observations and questions. Write down things that stand out to you, things that you notice, or things that you don't understand. Look up important words in a dictionary or interlinear Bible.

- Look for things like verbs, commands, and references to God. Notice key terms and themes throughout the passage.

- After you have worked through the text, read what is written in the study. Take time to look up any cross-references mentioned as you study.

- Then work through the questions provided in the book. Read and answer them prayerfully.

- Paraphrase or summarize the passage, or even just one verse from the passage. Putting it into your own words helps you to slow down and think through every word.

- Focus your heart on the character of God that you have seen in this passage. What do you learn about God from the passage you have studied? Adore Him and praise Him for who He is.

- Think and pray through application and how this passage should change you. Get specific with yourself. Resist the urge to apply the passage to others. Do you have sin to confess? How should this passage impact your attitude toward people or circumstances? Does the passage command you to do something? Do you need to trust Him for something in your life? How does the truth of the gospel impact your everyday life?

- We recommend you have a Bible, pen, highlighters, and journal as you work through this study. We recommend that ballpoint pens instead of gel pens be used in the study book to prevent smearing.

Here are several other optional resources that you may find helpful as you study:

WWW.BLUELETTERBIBLE.ORG

This free website is a great resource for digging deeper. You can find translation comparison, an interlinear option to look at words in the original languages, Bible dictionaries, and even commentary.

A DICTIONARY

If looking up words in the Hebrew and Greek feels intimidating, look up words in English. Often times we assume we know the meaning of a word, but looking it up and seeing its definition can help us understand a passage better.

A DOUBLE-SPACED COPY OF THE TEXT

You can use a website like www.biblegateway.com to copy the text of a passage and print out a double-spaced copy to be able to mark on easily. Circle, underline, highlight, draw arrows, and mark in any way you would like to help you dig deeper and work through a passage.

Introduction

The gospel is the good news of Jesus Christ that we need every single day. The gospel is for all of us because the gospel is for sinners—whether we are believers or unbelievers. We need the gospel for our salvation, but we also need it for every moment that follows. The gospel doesn't just give us grace at the moment of our conversion; the gospel gives us grace for all of life! From the mundane to the monumental, the gospel gives us hope and purpose and perspective. We can all attest to the reality that we are forgetful people. We quickly overlook the truth of the gospel in the everyday moments that make up our lives. We need to actively remind ourselves of God's grace. We need to daily declare to our own souls who God is and what He has done. We need to anchor our identities in Christ. We need to preach the gospel to ourselves daily.

What does preaching to your own soul look like? We can preach the gospel to ourselves by seeing the everyday moments in our lives through the lens of the person and work of Christ. We look to the Word of God to see what biblical principles He has given us in regard to the various aspects of our lives, from goals, to health, to relationships and more. 2 Peter 1:3 says, "His divine power has given us everything required for life and godliness through the knowledge of Him who called us by His own glory and goodness." Jesus gives us everything we need for life and godliness—this is the gospel. He is all we need! We need to know Him, not superficially, but intimately. We need to immerse ourselves in the gospel, in the knowledge of Him, and allow it to transform our everyday lives.

Our prayer is that this study will help equip you to meet every part of your life with gospel grace. In your families, may you grow in grace as God sanctifies you. In your work, may you see the gospel purpose in all your efforts. In your suffering, may you live in the hope of the resurrection. In all of life, may you be in awe of the holiness of our gracious God. We pray that your heart and mind would be saturated with the good news so that it permeates into every aspect of life. And may you always preach the gospel to yourself.

For His Glory,

Stefanie, Joanna, and
The Daily Grace Co. Team

"

Is there a better way?
Yes, and **the answer
is the gospel and
preaching the gospel
to yourself every day.**
The good news of saving
grace that led to your
saving faith is the good
news of sanctifying grace
that grows your faith.

table of contents

FOR FURTHER STUDY

*by grace alone through faith alone
in Jesus Christ alone*

What is the Gospel?

READ: GENESIS 3:15, ISAIAH 40, ROMANS 3:19-26

Begin by carefully reading today's Scripture passages. As you read through the passages, focus on the implications of the gospel for our past, present, and future.

Theologians call Genesis 3:15 the protoevangelium, which simply means the first gospel. But what is the gospel? The word gospel is the transliteration of the Greek word *euaggelion*, and it simply means good news, glad tidings, or joyous message. In the New Testament, the gospel is the message of salvation. But this Greek word *euaggelion* is not new. It is found in the Septuagint, the Greek translation of the Old Testament Jewish scrolls that were primarily written in Hebrew. So the Jews and Gentiles who were familiar with the scrolls would have recognized this word *euaggelion* that was proclaimed by the apostles. And their understanding would have been informed by Isaiah 40, which is an important passage where the prophet Isaiah wrote about the coming of the Messiah. Isaiah 40:9 says, "Zion, herald of good news, go up on a high mountain. Jerusalem, herald of good news, raise your voice loudly. Raise it, do not be afraid! Say to the cities of Judah, "Here is your God!"" And the good news follows in verses 10-11:

> *See, the Lord God comes with strength, and His power establishes His rule. His wages are with Him, and His reward accompanies Him. He protects His flock like a shepherd; He gathers the lambs in His arms and carries them in the fold of His garment. He gently leads those that are nursing. (Isaiah 40:10-11)*

The entire chapter magnifies the coming of the Messiah, Jesus Christ. And it was written at a time when the Israelites were in captivity; they were exiles in Babylon. So this was sweet news to them. Restoration would come for God's people! The Babylonian captivity ended after seventy years, just as He said. God made a way for His people to return to Jerusalem to rebuild the temple. But the ultimate restoration would come with Jesus, and He will be the King that ascends to "the throne of his father David, and He will reign over the house of Jacob forever, and of His kingdom there will be no end" (Luke 1:32-33).

Jesus is the gospel. He is the good news. And this is why Genesis 3:15 is the protoevangelium, or the first good news. As soon as God addressed Adam and Eve's disobedience and sin entered the world, He cursed the serpent. However, in the middle of the curse, God gave the message of hope. And this hope is Jesus. He is the one who will bruise the serpent's head and claim victory. This is good news! Adam and Eve's decision to eat of the fruit of the tree of knowledge of good and evil was not a simple act of disobedience. No, Adam and Eve's disobedience was an attempt to be god. It was an act of rebellion. They did not trust in God's goodness, provision, and authority. This is sin. It is disobedience, self-glorification, and unbelief. Sin goes against God's character, and the only just response to sin is judgment, the righteous wrath of God against sinners. And this is bad news because we are all sinners. Sin is a universal condition of mankind. As sinners, we are deserving of death (Romans 3:23, Romans 6:23). But the hope declared in Genesis 3:15 continues throughout the entire Bible. Every verse of Scripture points to the hope of the One that will rescue and redeem. Jesus is our hope. His work on the cross satisfied God's wrath. Jesus, the One we place our faith in, saves us! This is why we can simply say that the gospel is the good news about salvation that we receive by grace alone through faith alone in Jesus Christ alone.

But the gospel has implications for our past, present, and future because our salvation has past, present, and future realities. Our salvation is not limited to a single moment in time when we receive Jesus into our hearts by saying a scripted prayer. There is a moment of conversion when we put our faith in Christ. This is called *justification*. When we put our faith in Christ, the holiness required by the law is met because of Christ's holiness, and Jesus imputes His righteousness to us so that we are declared innocent. We are legally in right standing with God because of Jesus' life, death, and resurrection. We are free from the guilt of our sins forever. But we continue to experience our salvation in this life, and this is called *sanctification*. After our conversion, the Holy Spirit now indwells us and He begins to sanctify us—making us holy. He transforms us so that little by little we grow in holiness and are delivered from the power of sin. The Spirit empowers us to obey the Word of God and are conformed to the likeness of Jesus. Our sanctification is our present reality that will remain throughout our lives on this side of eternity. It is the grace of God toward us.

Lastly, the future reality of our salvation is our *glorification*. We are freed from the guilt of our sins and continually delivered from the power of sin, but the future reality that we greatly look forward to is when the presence of sin will be completely eradicated. Our glorification will be a work of God when He gathers His children to Himself. We will be raised from the dead and ushered into His kingdom with new, glorified bodies. In our glorification, our justification will match our sanctification! This is why the gospel is good news that offers an eternal gift, and it is freely offered to us by Jesus. We can behold Christ and find Him all-satisfying both now and forevermore.

This is the gospel.

1. THE GOSPEL IS THE MESSAGE OF SALVATION THROUGH JESUS CHRIST, AND IT IS THE STORY OF THE BIBLE. WHY IS IT GOOD NEWS?

2. IN YOUR OWN WORDS, WRITE OUT THE PAST, PRESENT, AND FUTURE REALITIES OF SALVATION.

3. WHAT IS THE RELATIONSHIP BETWEEN THE GOSPEL AND THE WAY THAT WE LIVE TODAY?

The gospel gives meaning to laughter and tears, and transforms hard hearts and hard days.

Why You Need The Gospel

READ: EPHESIANS 1:1-2:13, GALATIANS 2:19-20

Begin by carefully reading today's Scripture passages before coming back to this page. As you read through the passages, focus on the implications of the gospel for our past, present, and future.

Who needs the gospel? The answer to this question may seem obvious: those who are lost. Those who haven't heard it yet. Those who do not believe. All of these responses are correct, but they are not comprehensive. The gospel is not just for unbelievers. Believers need the gospel, too.

The gospel is not just something that matters for the moment of our salvation, although it certainly does, but the reach of the gospel extends to every single aspect of our lives, from the mundane to the monumental. As believers, the gospel is the lens through which we view the world; it is a set of glasses that allows the wearer to see God's beautiful plan for redemption woven into the nitty-gritty of life. The gospel promises purpose in confusion and joy in suffering. When we understand the beauty of the gospel, no area of our lives can go untouched by the hope and life that it brings.

When we come to a saving knowledge of the gospel and place our faith in Jesus Christ, we experience new birth as those who were dead in our sin but have now been made alive together with Christ by the love and mercy of the Father. But just as our salvation does not end with our justification, neither does our need for the gospel. We are not justified simply to escape hell and make it to heaven, but the new life that we now live we live to God, growing in holiness and obedience through the power of the Holy Spirit within us. The same grace that justified us is the very grace that sanctifies us and ultimately glorifies us, and we need the hope and power of the gospel for all of it. It is the gospel that declares us righteous by the righteousness of Christ, it is through the gospel that we are transformed into the glorious image of Jesus Christ, and it is the gospel that gives us purpose and perspective as we look to the consummation of our salvation when Christ returns.

Our need for the gospel does not only come into play in monumental moments, but also in the mundane. We need the gospel when we are lost and far from God, when tragedy strikes, and when we have a crisis of faith. But we also need the gospel when we brush our teeth, drive to work, and vacuum goldfish crackers out of a toddler's car seat. The gospel matters on Sunday mornings and Thursday afternoons. The gospel gives meaning to laughter and tears, and transforms hard hearts and hard days.

We need the gospel for all of life, and we are called to live all of life in light of the gospel. Paul reminds us along with the church in Ephesus to remember the gospel as we walk in the good works that God has prepared for us. When you feel lonely or out of place, remember that Christ gave His life to bring you close. When you feel too weak to turn from your sin, remember that Christ lives in you and empowers you to obey (Galatians 2:20). When you do mess up, remember that Christ's death means that there is no condemnation for you (Romans 8:1). When the circumstances of your life leave you asking, "Why me?" remember that your good and loving Father is working all things for your good, making you look like Jesus and preparing for you a glory that is far greater than any pain you are experiencing now (Romans 8:28, 2 Corinthians 3:18, 2 Corinthians 4:16-18).

The gospel gives the believer incredible freedom. Without Christ paying the penalty for our sins, our righteousness would be based entirely on our ability to follow God's law, but in Christ, we are free from the bonds of the law. Our salvation comes not from our own works, but the work of Jesus Christ. Therefore, we are freed to love and serve God and others, not to earn our salvation, but as an outpouring of the grace that we have been given. 1 John 4:19 declares that "we love because He first loved us." We are free to love our neighbors despite their sin, because Christ loved us in the midst of ours. We are free to cultivate habits of Bible study and prayer, not to earn God's favor, but to know and love Him more. The gospel frees us to be not good enough, or strong enough, or worthy enough, because Christ is our sufficiency, and when we are weak, He is strong in us (2 Corinthians 12:9-11).

As those who have been freed by the gospel, we live all of life according to the gospel as good stewards of God's grace in every area of our lives. All of Scripture and all of history is centered around the good news of Jesus Christ, and it ought to be the center of our lives too.

We are free to love our neighbors despite their sin, because Christ loved us in the midst of ours. We are free to cultivate habits of Bible study and prayer, not to earn God's favor, but to know and love Him more.

1. ACCORDING TO EPHESIANS 1:1-2:13, WHAT IMPACT DOES THE GOSPEL HAVE ON A BELIEVER'S PAST, PRESENT AND FUTURE?

_____

_____

_____

_____

_____

2. DO YOU LIVE ALL OF LIFE IN LIGHT OF THE GOSPEL? WHAT ARE SOME AREAS IN YOUR LIFE THAT YOU TEND TO VIEW APART FROM THE GOSPEL?

_____

_____

_____

_____

_____

3. BASED ON GALATIANS 2:19-20, HOW DOES THE DEATH AND RESURRECTION OF CHRIST TRANSFORM THE WAY WE LIVE OUR EVERYDAY LIVES?

_____

_____

_____

_____

_____

*We simply reflect Him in such a way
as to show others who He is.*

The Gospel and the Glory of God

READ: JOHN 15:1-17, I CORINTHIANS 10:23-33

Begin by carefully reading today's Scripture passage. As you read through the passage, consider the metaphor Jesus uses and identify who Jesus says is the vine, the vinedresser, and the branches.

Catechisms are helpful resources to learn the teachings of the Christian faith. The very first question and answer set in the Westminster Shorter Catechism is this: *What is the chief end of man?* Man's chief end is to glorify God, and to enjoy him forever. There is no confusion. God made human beings to bring Him glory. But what does that mean? What exactly is God's glory? Is His glory dependent on us? What are the practical implications of glorifying God?

It's important to know the nature of the glory of God. It is intrinsic. God's glory is all of His attributes on display. It's who He is. Having a proper understanding of God's glory makes it abundantly obvious that it is not dependent on us. Finite beings cannot add to an infinite God. However, God created us to glorify Him. How can we glorify God when we cannot add to or take away from His glory? Psalm 19:1 states, "The heavens declare the glory of God, and the expanse proclaims the work of His hands." The vast universe, composed of billions of galaxies, glorifies God because it displays His infinity. Have you seen photos of the universe taken by the Hubble telescope? They are breathtaking, aren't they? These images simply reflect the greatness of the Creator! All of creation reveals the glory of God, the Creator.

Since what can be known about God is evident among them, because God has shown it to them. For his invisible attributes, that is, his eternal power and divine nature, have been clearly seen since the creation of the world, being understood through what He has made. As a result, people are without excuse. (Romans 1:19-20)

These verses tell us that the vast beauty found in nature is God's natural revelation of Himself. Countless galaxies and the most beautiful mountain ranges and breathtaking sunrises and sunsets are His fingerprints. Nature simply reflects the greatness of God because of the way God made them. And this is what it means for us to glorify God. We simply reflect Him in such a way as to show others who He is. We were created to show the world how supremely great our Creator is, and He gave us the capacity to do this because He made us His image bearers (Genesis 1:26). Is it not amazing how God perfectly crafted His creation to align with their purpose?

All human beings are image bearers, and God's desire is for all men to be saved (1 Timothy 2:4, 2 Peter 2:9). The purpose of humanity is to glorify God. How do we do this? Jesus said in John 15:8, "My Father is glorified by this: that you produce much fruit and prove to be My disciples." Jesus used the metaphor of the vine and branches in this passage in order to establish the basis of Christian living. In this metaphor, Jesus is the vine and there are two types of branches that are differentiated by their fruit. Branches that bear fruit are genuine believers, and the bearing of fruit is what brings God glory. But in the Christian life, what does this fruit look like?

The Greek word for fruit in this verse is *karpos*. It is the same word used in James 3:18 in regard to the fruit of righteousness. This type of fruit is produced by God's righteousness in the life of a believer and refers to good works. Our good works are evidence of our faith; they are a testimony of our union with Christ. It is a life of excellence. It is a life where word, thought, and deed align with the Word. It is a life that is characterized by the fruit of the Spirit (Galatians 5:22-23). This fruit is also leading someone to Christ, obeying the command to make disciples (Matthew 28:19). All believers are instructed to proclaim the excellencies of Christ (1 Peter 2:9)!

Does this kind of fruit bearing life sound impossible? Remember the metaphor of the vine and branches in John 15. Jesus is the true vine. He is the source of life and fruitfulness. And God the Father is the vinedresser. He tends to the vine and the branches to bear all of the fruit that He intends. Jesus explained the proper order clearly in John 15:5, "I am the vine; you are the branches. The one who re-mains in Me and I in him produces much fruit, because you can do nothing without Me." We simply need to abide in Him. But how do we abide in Christ? Jesus tells us a few verses later to keep His commandments. This may sound legalistic, but it's not. Our obedience to His Word is an expression of our love. Our love for God and others covers our entire moral duty (Matthew 22:10). Our love can be expressed in trust, belief, prayer, obedience, service, and more. And this love relationship produces joy and satisfaction.

We can glorify God moment by moment by abiding in Him, loving and enjoying Him, and allowing the Spirit to sanctify us to better image Him. Glorifying God through our lives is not limited to Christian activities but extends to the whole of our lives. The Apostle Paul reminds us in 1 Corinthians 10:31 that we have freedom in Christ. We are not bound by cere-monial rules; we have the liberty to eat, drink, and out of that freedom we "do everything for the glory of God." In our freedom in Christ, we should seek the good of others in order to build them up. In our freedom in Christ, we walk in joyful obedience as we seek to glorify God in all things. This is how our mundane tasks can glorify God. In the ordinary rou-tines of our lives, we can show the world His glory by bending low, serving, and loving with joy and true humility, mirroring Christ. We preach the gospel to ourselves everyday to re-mind us of these truths!

1. BASED ON TODAY'S PASSAGE, HOW DOES JESUS' METAPHOR OF THE VINE AND BRANCHES INFORM THE WAY WE LIVE TODAY?

2. WHAT IS GOD'S GLORY? WHAT IS THE PROPER RESPONSE TO GOD'S GLORY?

3. WE CAN GLORIFY GOD BY BEARING GOOD FRUIT. WHAT DOES IT LOOK LIKE TO BEAR GOOD FRUIT IN THE CHRISTIAN LIFE?

The gospel should be the lens through which believers see their lives.

The Gospel for Goals & Decisions

READ: EPHESIANS 5:15-21, GALATIANS 5:13-25, ROMANS 8:1-17

Begin by carefully reading today's Scripture passages. Focus on the differences noted between the flesh and the Spirit in the various passages.

Many people like to set goals each year. This typically happens at the new year, but it can occur at different stages throughout the year. You may feel motivated to make positive changes. We like the idea to start fresh and to accomplish something that we feel like we need to accomplish. But it is also a reality that many people burn out before they reach this goal. You may wonder if you'll fall into that latter category. The excitement dwindles when you do not consistently meet daily and weekly goals. Discouragement creeps in and you doubt that it's even possible to make positive changes at all. Are we hopeless in this cause?

It is helpful to dig deeper here. What is the aim of our goals? Why are we pursuing betterment in a particular area? What is the motivating factor? To whom are we looking to sustain our efforts? These are important questions to ask ourselves and to answer. This is also why this study started with the gospel and our need for the gospel. The truth is, the gospel is the answer to all of the above because the gospel is for the whole of our lives. As we read earlier this week, the gospel extends to every single aspect of our lives from the mundane to the monumental. The gospel should be the lens through which believers see their lives. When it is, the gospel interprets everything we think, feel, and perceive in this world. When it comes to our goals, the gospel compels us because it reminds us that we are stewards of God's grace in every area of our lives.

But what does it mean to be a steward? A steward is someone that is entrusted with someone else's resources. They are responsible for whatever is given to them. Believers are called "good stewards of God's varied grace" (1 Peter 4:10). God, according to His grace, gives His children gifts. They are completely unearned. And the primary purpose of these gifts is to serve one another. Our particular gifts can be viewed as God's provision. He equips us to fulfill the role in the body of Christ that He has for us. And ultimately, it is for His glory.

But what about the nitty-gritty details of our lives? What about our particular goals and the thousands of decisions we have to make every single day? Can the gospel inform those areas of our lives? The answer is yes. When it comes to the ends of the spectrum of right and wrong, Scripture leaves no room for questioning. It is explicitly clear on sin, and there are many passages that show us God's desire for how His people should live. But the spectrum is wide, and the majority of our goals and decisions fall in between. When our goals and decisions are not explicitly deemed as right or wrong in Scripture, it is helpful to move forward with the principles in Scripture serving as our guidelines. This is why it's important to know the Word of God in its entirety and to allow this knowledge to be the most compelling force in the making of our goals and decisions.

But before forming resolutions, it's important to begin with repentance. We are not enough on our own. We cannot transform ourselves into the likeness of Christ. We cannot produce holiness on our own no matter how resolved we are. We need Jesus, and as believers, we have the indwelling Holy Spirit. He empowers us to overcome the power of sin in our lives, and He sanctifies us. From there, we lean on the principles in Scripture to craft personal resolutions. We strive to make our goals and decisions align with His Word and His purpose.

God's aim for His image bearers is to bring Him glory, and the way to bring Him the most glory is to be completely satisfied in Him. There is freedom in Christ. We are no longer bound to our sins and powerless to the whims of our flesh. We can live joyfully in the newness of life that Christ offers in the tension of the "already,

but not yet," which simply recognizes that we will continue to struggle with the flesh on this side of eternity but we are not alone. We have His Spirit, and we have the church. And we look forward to the "not yet"—the certain future that we have in Jesus where evil will be completely eradicated and He will dwell with His people forever! And this is the future that we keep in mind when making our goals and decisions—the future reality of eternity, not the next calendar year.

Don't let the details paralyze you or plunge you into hopelessness. As you're able, simply filter your goals and decisions through a few questions: *Is this goal or decision going to cultivate godliness? Will it equip me to better reflect Christ? Will it bring me into bondage of sin? Is it a weight that God has called me to bear at this time? Will it be a means to encourage fellow believers? Would Jesus do it?* Prayerfully consider these things and then make goals. Make decisions with confidence! It's helpful to use practical tools like the SMART method—to make resolutions that are Specific, Measurable, Attainable, Realistic, and Timely. But when it comes down to it, keep it simple. Be satisfied in Christ. Obey His Word. Love Him and love your neighbors. And live the life that He has given you.

The gospel is for the whole of our lives.

1. BASED ON TODAY'S PASSAGES, WHAT PRINCIPLES CAN YOU IDENTIFY THAT CAN GUIDE YOU IN YOUR GOALS AND DECISION MAKING?

2. HOW DOES THE GOSPEL OFFER YOU FREEDOM IN YOUR GOALS AND DECISION MAKING?

3. HOW WOULD YOUR GOALS CHANGE IF THEY WERE WRITTEN WITH ETERNITY IN MIND?

*Without the gospel, there is neither spiritual life
nor spiritual flourishing.*

The Gospel for Spiritual Health

READ: ROMANS 6, TITUS 2:11-14

Begin by carefully reading today's Scripture passages before coming back to this page. As you read through the passages, focus on the connection between our salvation and the way we should live.

The gospel is absolutely vital for our spiritual health. Without the gospel, there is neither spiritual life nor spiritual flourishing. There is no spiritual life that does not result in spiritual growth. We know that when we are justified, God declares us to be righteous. He frees us from the penalty of sin and calls us holy. If this is our standing before God, why do we need spiritual growth? If we are not saved by good works, then why spend so much time and effort trying to do them? The good news of the gospel is that Jesus did not die to save us only from the penalty of sin, but also from the power of sin. Christ gave His very life to make us new, a sacrifice too costly and precious to scorn by continuing to walk in the very sin He shed His blood to overcome. God not only calls us sons, He makes us look like the Son. God doesn't just call us new creations, He transforms us bit by bit into something holy. God not only declares us righteous, He makes us righteous. God creates and sanctifies what He calls.

Every aspect of our lives, when centered on the gospel, contributes to our spiritual health, but it is the personal spiritual disciplines that specifically and uniquely produce the fruit of holiness in the life of the believer. There are many spiritual disciplines, including fasting, worship, evangelism, service, journaling, solitude, learning, and stewardship, but the two most important ones in the life of the believer are Bible study and prayer. All the other disciplines flow out of these.

As we behold the glory of the Lord, we are actually transformed into His image (2 Corinthians 3:18). We become what we behold. So if we are to grow in sanctification, we must gaze upon the glory of God, and the primary way that God reveals Himself and His glory is through His Word. The Word of God includes the written Word, which is the Scripture, and the incarnate Word, who is Jesus Christ (John 1:14). All of Scripture points to Christ, and so it is in the Bible that we most fully and clearly see the glory of God revealed. When we make ingesting God's Word a daily discipline, we are transformed day by day, bit by bit, degree by degree into righteousness. As we read God's Word, we see who He is. We come to know Him and love Him and even look like Him. This discipline is not just a discipline of reading, but of meditating. This type of meditation is not in the sense of emptying our minds, but filling it with the truth of God's Word. Meditating on a passage of Scripture takes our study of God's Word from head knowledge to personal knowledge of the Creator. It moves from information to transformational application.

When we pray, we respond to who God is as He has revealed Himself in His Word. We worship Him for what He has done. We confess how we have fallen short of His glory. We seek His help in every area of our lives. In prayer, we commune with God as we communicate with Him, and as we pray, God aligns our hearts to His. For the believer, prayer is both a discipline and a way of life. Colossians 4:2 instructs us to devote ourselves to prayer, indicating that it is an intentional, disciplined action. We ought to have focused times of prayer daily where we approach God undistracted by each day's responsibilities. Just as Jesus modeled in the gospels, we should retreat daily from work and play and to-do lists to speak with our Father.

Many of us know that we should read our Bibles and pray, and we are overcome with guilt because we don't do it enough. Others of us diligently study and pray every day, confident that God is pleased with us because of our devotion. Others still lack any regular discipline of Bible study and prayer, believing them to be unnecessary because of the grace that God so freely lavishes on us. All three of these approaches fail to see spiritual disciplines in light of the gospel. The first two approaches tend toward legalism, which is the belief that we somehow earn our salvation or favor with God by our works. It is a belief that either produces guilt for inevitably falling short or unwarranted pride in thinking we are good enough to live up to God's standards. The third tends toward apathy that stems from the idea that because Christ has paid it all, nothing more is required of us, a belief that ignores God's commands to be holy as He is holy. This belief leads us to God when it is convenient, when we feel like it, or when we need something, but not in any kind of disciplined way.

The gospel frees us from approaching spiritual disciplines with legalism or apathy. Ephesians 2:8-9 tells us that our salvation is a gift from God given to us by His grace, and we can never earn any part of it by our works. We have favor with God because we have been given the righteousness of Christ, not because we earned it. Therefore, the quality or frequency of our spiritual disciplines should be neither a source of pride nor of condemnation. This passage goes on to explain that our salvation should result in good works. God has prepared good works for us, and He empowers us to walk in them by the Holy Spirit who now dwells within us.

And so we come to Him, not to earn His love or for a feel-good pick-me-up, but to be holy as He is holy. We seek Him in His Word and through prayer with the joy and freedom that comes from being called children of God, willingly giving our lives to the One who gave His life for us.

1. BASED ON TODAY'S PASSAGES, WHAT IS THE RELATIONSHIP BETWEEN THE GOSPEL AND THE WAY THAT WE LIVE?

2. DO YOU TEND MORE TO LEGALISM OR APATHY WHEN IT COMES TO SPIRITUAL DISCIPLINES?

3. HOW DOES THE GOSPEL TRANSFORM THE WAY WE APPROACH BIBLE STUDY AND PRAYER?

I have been crucified with Christ, and I no longer live, but Christ lives in me. The life I now live in the body, I live by faith in the Son of God, who loved me and gave himself for me.

GALATIANS 2:20

WEEK I *reflection*

PARAPHRASE THE PASSAGES FROM THIS WEEK.

_____
_____
_____
_____
_____
_____
_____
_____
_____
_____
_____
_____

WHAT DID YOU OBSERVE FROM THIS WEEK'S TEXT ABOUT
GOD AND HIS CHARACTER?

_____
_____
_____
_____
_____
_____

WHAT DO THESE PASSAGES TEACH ABOUT THE CONDITION OF
MANKIND AND ABOUT YOURSELF?

_____
_____
_____
_____
_____
_____
_____
_____

HOW DO THESE PASSAGES POINT TO THE GOSPEL?

HOW SHOULD YOU RESPOND TO THESE PASSAGES?
WHAT IS THE PERSONAL APPLICATION?

WHAT SPECIFIC ACTION STEPS CAN YOU TAKE THIS WEEK
TO APPLY THESE PASSAGES?

Looking to the eternal gives perspective for the temporary.

The Gospel for the Overwhelmed Heart

READ: PSALM 34; MATTHEW 6:25-24, MATTHEW 11:28-30, GALATIANS 4:6-7

Begin by carefully reading today's Scripture passages before coming back to this page. As you read through the passages, focus on what the gospel has to say about our worries and fears.

Most of us have a pretty standard response to the question, "How was your week?" The answer? "Busy!" As we juggle all of the day's responsibilities and to-do lists, the unknowns and the things out of our control, the pitfalls and failures, and all the people vying for our time and attention, it is easy to become overwhelmed. Even if you don't have a busy schedule, you are not exempt from a busy mind. Before you know it, you find yourself overwhelmed and anxious and stripped of your joy.

Restless hearts can be a sign that we have forgotten the gospel. The gospel has answers for our past mistakes. It offers hope for our present struggles. It gives assurance for our future.

When our past mistakes swirl around in our minds and the constant spinning makes us nauseous, we have forgotten the good news that in Christ we are clean. Christ's work on the cross does not just pay the penalty for our sin, although that alone is a gift of immeasurable grace, but in Christ we also gain the imputed righteousness of the Son of God. Being in Christ, then, means that we do not have to dwell on the mistakes of yesterday, because Christ's blood has washed them away. It

means that we don't have to sit in our shame because there is no condemnation for those who are in Christ (Romans 8:1). It means that it is pointless to agonize over what we should have done differently, because Christ will make all things new. God is not limited by our mistakes. He will accomplish all His good purposes.

When we are overwhelmed by the never-ending lists of things that have to be done, we are forgetting that those who hope in the gospel set their minds on eternal things. Not that we neglect our responsibilities, but that we do them with the perspective that the things of this world are transient. They are passing away. That huge pile of laundry that needs to be folded, those meals that need to be planned, that medical bill that needs to be paid, none of that will matter ten billion years from now or maybe even ten years from now! So why do we let our minds and hearts be troubled by temporary things? There are things that will still be around ten billion years from now and for eternity—our triune God, our inheritance in Christ, the Word of God, our brothers and sisters in Christ—aren't these the things worth setting our minds on? Like Martha who is too anxious about cooking and cleaning to stop and sit at the feet of Jesus (Luke 10:38-42), we are prone to let our stress about our daily tasks avert our gaze from the things that last for eternity. Looking to the eternal gives perspective for the temporary.

When we feel discouraged because we are at the end of ourselves and have nothing left to give, we are forgetting the good news that those who are in Christ have the Spirit of Christ within them. It may be true that we reach the end of our own strength, but our response should not be dejection, but rejoicing! It is when we come to the end of ourselves that Christ's power is made perfect in us (2 Corinthians 12:9). His grace is sufficient, so we need not fear failure as a result of our own weakness. Even at our strongest we are never enough, and even at our weakest Christ is more than enough. It is when our own limited resources are depleted that we can rest in unhindered dependence on the source of all our strength. So rejoice in sleepless nights with sick children! Rejoice in the unexpected wrenches that get thrown into your perfectly planned day! It is far better to be filled with the power of God in our weakness than it is to live out of the frailty of our greatest strength.

When we are fearful of what the future holds, we are forgetting the good news that our good God and Father is sovereign over all. Because of Christ, all of God's sovereign power is for us, working all things together for our good (Romans 8:28). He is in control of the future, but we often live our lives as if we are in control. We pass our days worrying about our kids, our jobs, our health, our safety, as if our concern will somehow change the outcome—and all the while "Our God is in heaven and does whatever he pleases" (Psalm 115:3). In our fear we not only live under the illusion that we are in control, we also desperately desire that control. But that kind of responsibility is a burden too heavy for us to bear. God is good. God is in control. God is for you. God will do what is right.

The gospel offers hope for our restless souls. Our Savior invites us to come and lay our burdens on Him, because He has already paid the price for them all. He invites us to come to His Word to hear the gospel every day. He invites us to come to Him in prayer with all of our worries and fears, knowing that our Father in Heaven cares for us. When we lay our heads on our pillow, instead of tossing and turning, overcome with worries and fears, we can say as the psalmist says: "I will both lie down and sleep in peace, for you alone, Lord, make me live in safety" (Psalm 4:8).

The gospel has answers for our past mistakes.
It offers hope for our present struggles.
It gives assurance for our future.

1. WHAT DOES PSALM 34 REVEAL ABOUT GOD? HOW DOES THIS PSALM GIVE YOU HOPE FOR YOUR FEARS?

2. WHAT AREAS OF YOUR LIFE DO YOU TEND TO WORRY OR BECOME OVERWHELMED ABOUT? HOW DOES THE GOSPEL CONFRONT THOSE FEELINGS?

3. WHAT PRACTICAL STEPS CAN YOU TAKE TO COMBAT ANXIETY IN YOUR OWN LIFE WITH THE GOSPEL?

He is our Creator, the divine Designer.

The Gospel for Physical Health

READ: I TIMOTHY 4:6-16, I CORINTHIANS 9:24-27, I CORINTHIANS 10:23-11:1

Begin by carefully reading today's Scripture passages before coming back to this page. As you read through the passages, focus on what the gospel has to say about your body.

Many people are concerned with their physical health. We latch on to the latest exercise trend or diet. This tendency is evident in the fact that the diet industry is worth over $70 billion. Grocery store aisles are littered with magazines raving about the new diet or exercise regiment that guarantees to shed pounds. There are new apps and workout subscription programs advertised on every corner of the internet. There are always new gyms opening up across town. And in regards to nutrition, the amount of information on the varying theories and tailored diets is insurmountable. But why is it that government data still claims that nearly 70 percent of adults in the U.S. are overweight or obese? Something is amiss. The obsession with physical fitness and proper nutrition is not working. It's not the answer. But how does the gospel speak to this valid issue of diet and exercise? Aside from detailed diet rules in the Old Testament that we are no longer bound to, does the Bible have anything to say about our physical well being?

Remember, God made us—body and soul. And in His work of redemption, He redeems the whole person—body and soul. The glorification that we look forward to includes a new resurrected body. But how are we instructed to care for our physical bodies right now? The Apostle Paul said this:

Train yourself in godliness. For the training of the body has limited benefit, but godliness is beneficial in every way, since it holds promise for the present life and also for the life to come.
(1 Timothy 4:7-8)

Bodily training has limited benefit. The driving principle is this: godliness is more valuable because it will last for all of eternity. The determined worth of anything is influenced by its permanency. This is why the value of our physical fitness is limited. It won't extend beyond this earth. But there is value for the here and now. Taking care of our bodies with regular exercise and nutritious food can allow us to be better stewards. Physical wellbeing can lead to mental clarity, allowing us to study the Word of God and engage with our neighbors. It can also lead to more strength and energy to serve others, where our acts of service are an expression of our love for God. In these ways, the conditioning of our bodies, accomplished through food and exercise, is done to glorify God. We heed Paul's instruction in 1 Corinthians 10:31, "So, whether you eat or drink, or whatever you do, do everything for the glory of God".

However, we must be careful. Our mortal bodies (which includes the mind) are vulnerable to sin because our flesh is unredeemed (Romans 6:12). Paul says he disciplines his body and keeps it under control (1 Corinthians 9:27). There is a daily battle between our flesh and the Spirit (Galatians 5:17). It is not hard to see that diet and exercise can be gateways to sin. Our world is obsessed with external beauty. Many tether identity and self-worth to body image. This mindset drives the discipline of many to adhere to a particular diet and log in a specific number of hours at the gym a day. But believers are to exercise a different sort of discipline. Spiritual disciplines prioritize the study of God's word, prayer, fasting, and worship. The Holy Spirit bears the fruit of self-control, which is the discipline of restraining our passions and appetites. This restraint lends to a new set of priorities that allocates time in a way to glorify God. Instead of working out ninety minutes a day, perhaps it is reduced to thirty minutes with the sole intention of devoting an hour to His Word, prayer, and serving someone in need.

It is a battle of affections in our hearts. What are we treasuring? What are we beholding? This is the issue of gluttony, which is simply an overindulgence of food. But it can also be a clothing size or a half-marathon time. And the primary way to overcome these competing desires is to be conquered by a greater desire. It is to treasure Christ and be all-satisfied in Him. It is to look to Him for comfort, not endorphins or chocolate cake. It is to look to Him for self-worth, not a particular physique achieved by diet and exercise. He is our Creator, the divine Designer.

And according to His perfect design, He made our bodies to need rest. Although we are not under the law of the Sabbath, believers are encouraged to practice the Lord's Day. We worship with fellow believers in the local church, and it is our spiritual rest as we encourage one another, worship Christ's finished work, and look forward to our eternal rest when He returns (Hebrews 10:25). We also physically rest, acknowledging our limited nature. In a culture where busyness is glorified, acknowledging the Lord's day is radical. Yet, as people with our eyes fixed on eternity and our identities anchored in Christ, it is an exercise of reverence. It is a pattern of rest set forth in the Word of God, and it is contrary to the self-care gospel that overwhelms our world today. We want to care for our bodies because they are living temples of God, but this is not accomplished in self-care as the world asserts. No, true rest is not offered in treating ourselves or retreating from our lives to be refilled. We are united with Jesus, the living water, who offers continual refreshment and renewal of strength (John 4:10, Isaiah 40:31). And in turn, we bend lower and serve others better, as if we were serving the Lord (Colossians 3:23). We apply the gospel to our bodies when we confess that they're limited, imperfect, and not divine. And in the gospel, we find Christ who is all-satisfying and worthy of our worship.

1. IN TODAY'S PASSAGE, WE READ THAT BODILY TRAINING HAS SOME VALUE, BUT GODLINESS IS THE BETTER PORTION WITH LASTING VALUE. HOW DOES THAT CHANGE YOUR THOUGHTS ON DIET AND EXERCISE?

2. THERE IS NOTHING INHERENTLY WRONG WITH DIETING AND EXERCISING. HOWEVER, IT IS A BATTLE OF OUR AFFECTIONS. WHAT ARE THE DOMINATING AFFECTIONS IN YOUR HEART? HOW DO THESE AFFECTIONS TRANSLATE INTO YOUR RESOLUTIONS?

3. HOW DOES THE GOSPEL APPLY TO OUR BODIES?

HOW WE VIEW THEM:

HOW WE CARE FOR THEM:

HOW WE USE THEM:

*Jesus Christ gave His very life to
make us His own.*

The Gospel for Marriage & Singleness

READ: MATTHEW 19:5-6, EPHESIANS 5:22-33, I PETER 3:1-9, REVELATION 19:6-9

Begin by carefully reading today's Scripture passages before coming back to this page. As you read through the passages, focus on how the gospel informs our understanding of marriage.

The hope of every believer is marriage. Many women dream of the day when they will walk down the aisle in a white dress into their happily ever after, but that is not the kind of marriage I am talking about. Our ultimate hope is not in a husband and wife becoming one flesh, but in being united with Christ, the true bridegroom. Jesus Christ is preparing for Himself a pure and spotless bride, the church, who will be united to Him as the very body of Christ. Jesus Christ gave His very life to make us His own, even in the midst of our infidelity and love affair with sin. All who are believers in Christ are betrothed to Him, and He is preparing and sanctifying His bride for the wedding feast of the Lamb when Christ returns and we—His church, His bride, His body—will be holy and blameless and eternally united with Him in glory.

As the body of Christ, we are called to put the gospel on display in our lives. God has given marriage as a picture of the relationship between Christ and the church, and it is Christ's love for the church that is to be a model for our marriage relationships. Husbands are called to love their wives as Christ loves the church. This kind of love is not self-seeking but self-sacrificial. It is a love that endures even when sinned against. It is a love that gives it's very life for the bride. The husband has the weighty call of protecting, loving, and leading his wife, not to be her savior, but to point her and the watching world to the true Savior who is coming for His bride. All of Scripture and all of history is pointing to Jesus, and marriage is no exception.

Wives are called to submit to their husbands even as their husbands submit to Christ. This kind of submission imitates the humility of Christ, willingly submitting to God's plan and will for our good and protection. God's vision for marriage is not one where a husband uses his strength to dominate his wife as he rules over her, but one in which the husband uses his strength to protect, nurture, and honor his wife. Wives submit to their husbands' leadership, knowing that ultimately they are submitting to God who has established this order for marriage. This kind of humility and submission to God's design is a powerful testimony to the beauty and love of the gospel, a picture that God may use even to bring unbelievers to Himself, including unbelieving husbands (1 Peter 3:1).

It is important to note that submission to husbands should never mean submission to sin.

A husband may ask his wife to do something that she does not want to do, such as move to a new city, attend a particular church, or send their kids to a certain school, and in these things wives are ultimately called to submit to the final decision of their husbands. However, wives should not submit to requests from their husbands to sin, such as watch pornography, be dishonest on tax returns, or cease to worship God.

Human marriage is a pointer to our marriage to Christ, but the two are not equal. The marriage we experience on this side of eternity is flawed and full of conflict because it is a union between two sinful people. Many of us, whether married or single, make the mistake of elevating a spouse to the position of savior, believing that we will be truly happy and fulfilled when and only when we find our soulmate. If we look to our imperfect spouse as the source of our happiness, we will be horribly disappointed. A spouse cannot save you. Only Jesus can do that. A husband or wife cannot fulfill all your desires. Only God can do that. It is unfair, unprofitable, and idolatrous to put the weight of your happiness on someone who was never meant to fulfill your needs.

For those who are single, this means you do not have to wait for a spouse before you can live a life of fruitful service to Christ and abundant joy in His love. You may hope to be married, and that desire can be healthy, but you are not incomplete in your singleness, because you have everything you need in your union with Christ. You do not need a spouse—you need Jesus.

For those who are married, the understanding that our satisfaction and salvation comes from God alone ought to change the way we respond to conflict within marriage. Christ is preparing His bride for Himself by sanctifying her, and one way that He sanctifies us is through our human marriages. Too often, we leave a marriage simply because we are unhappy, believing that the goal of marriage is our personal fulfillment. However, God's purpose in marriage is not to make us happy, but to make us holy. When your spouse is not showing you the affection you long for, rather than turn to someone else to fulfill those unmet desires, turn to God who satisfies all your needs. When your spouse sins against you, rather than retaliate in anger or frustration, praise God for the opportunity to be an ambassador of God's grace to your spouse. When your spouse is selfishly seeking their own good over yours, rather than fight for what you think you deserve, seek to outdo your spouse in showing love and honor (Romans 12:10).

Whether you are married or single, marriage is a pointer that should direct your gaze and your hope to the marriage supper of the Lamb, when we all, as the body of Christ, will be presented to Him as His pure and spotless bride. This marriage is the only one that promises full and complete joy and satisfaction.

1. HOW DOES THE GOSPEL INFORM YOUR UNDERSTANDING OF MARRIAGE?

2. DO YOU FIND YOURSELF PUTTING THE BURDEN OF YOUR HAPPINESS ON A SPOUSE OR OTHER PERSON?

3. RE-READ REVELATION 19:6-9. HOW CAN YOU FIND HOPE IN MARRIAGE WHETHER YOU ARE MARRIED OR SINGLE?

Parenting is a God-given calling and the Lord is using you to form a human soul.

The Gospel for Parenthood & Discipleship

READ: DEUTERONOMY 6:4-9, 20-23

Begin by carefully reading today's Scripture passages before coming back to this page. As you read through the passages, think of the potential practical implications of these verses in regard to parenting.

Simply put, parenting is hard. It doesn't matter if you've been entrusted with one teenager or five kids under the age of eight. Meeting the practical demands to sustain life requires a lot of sacrifice and energy and repetition. And on top of meeting those everyday needs, you have the desire to nurture their hearts and help them navigate their emotions. As you potty train and help resolve conflict with kind words instead of fists, you want to help them know and cherish the Word of God. You want them to excel in school and extracurricular activities and experience the beauty of being a part of the local church. The menial tasks of parenthood are endless, yet there are also the emotional and spiritual needs that require development! Sometimes, you may want to give up. But remember this: parenting is a God-given calling and the Lord is using you to form a human soul. This may sound intimidating. You may wonder if it is even possible to do it well. But the answer to being an effective tool in the lives of our children is to always keep the big picture of the gospel in mind. The gospel reminds us that it is Him who works from start to finish. The gospel reminds us that the goal is His glory and that's the only measure of success. Whatever season of parenting you are in, your greatest need is not found in a specific strategy or formula. No, your every need is fully met in the gospel.

Our children don't belong to us. They were created by God for His purpose. They are His possession, and parents are entrusted with these blessings from the Lord. Being entrusted with something that is not yours means you're a steward. The better title in parenting is ambassador — as parents, we are Christ's ambassadors. Your role as an ambassador is simple: to represent the One who sent you. This is your purpose regardless of if you are a parent or not. To represent the One who sent you — to put His message, values, and character on display — is simply to give Him glory. And as we've learned, the chief end of man is to glorify God. As parents, we have the unique opportunity to glorify Him in the realm of raising children. However, even if we do not have the responsibility of raising children, we are still called to make disciples, and making disciples is essentially spiritual parenting! We are called to teach the next generation to love His Word, trust Him, and obey Him. The Apostle Paul, who didn't have any biological children, had many spiritual children. He called Timothy his "beloved son" in the faith in the salutations to both letters written to

Timothy. And he called Titus "my true child in a common faith" (Titus 1:4).

But what does glorifying God as His ambassador look like in the nitty-gritty details of parenting? The Bible doesn't go into great length about it. Maybe that's why there are over 75,000 books on parenting in the market today! People want instructional how-to books; however, rather than serving as supplements to the Bible, they have become replacements. But here's the truth: the Bible offers all of the principles you need to parent your child as God intends. Consider today's Bible passage—in ten verses, we are offered the framework to sufficiently guide us in the monumental task of raising children. First, we are to love God and the expression of our love should be obedience to His Word. Then we are to teach the Word of God to our children in every life circumstance and season. Rather than tying boxes with verses on our foreheads (v. 8), we are to have a Bible-saturated worldview where God and His Word are the filter through which we see everything in life. Modeling and teaching this biblical worldview is a means through which God will shape our children to glorify Him.

God's primary concern is not whether or not our child participates in travel baseball. It is not whether or not our child grows up to be a doctor or an engineer. His primary concern is the affections of our child's heart. The teaching of His Word is a means to protect them against idol worship. Consider the Israelites—after Joshua led them into the Promised Land, that generation died. The Bible says in Judges 2:10 that the next generation did not "know the Lord or the work that He had done for Israel". The next verse clearly reveals the repercussions of this lack of

instruction from their parents: the Israelites "did evil in the eyes of the Lord and served the Baals." They forsook God and "followed and worshiped various gods of the peoples around them." We are after our children's hearts. We want them to know, love, and worship the living God! And as we give guidance and teach our children about idolatry, submission to authority, and character, we are showing them their need for a Savior. This is how we are a tool used by God as His ambassador.

As God uses us in our children's lives, He uses our children to grow us as well. Our good Father is after our hearts. This is seen in how He uses parenthood to sanctify us. In His brilliant design, He has allowed the intricacies of parenthood to be a sort of mirror to show us our weaknesses, sin tendencies, and need for Him. Is it not true that a gift of having a newborn is realizing how self-centered and selfish we are? The very real frustration over our helpless newborn's sleep pattern or eating schedule shows us how tightly we hold onto our preferences! When our 3-year old throws a tantrum or our pre-teen complains incessantly or our teenager shows apathy or annoyance, we are reminded of our own heart attitudes before our Father. We grumble and complain, we seek self-comfort over obedience, and we throw a tantrum that He is not doing things our way. And this is a gift. It is His grace. And as we lean into Him in these moments of weakness and frustration and introspection, we confess our need for Him. We pray for His Holy Spirit to empower us to overcome our sins and to better reflect our Father. And as we are sanctified and learn more about our God, we teach the next generation to do the same.

1. TODAY'S PASSAGES CAN SERVE AS A SUFFICIENT FRAMEWORK TO GUIDE OUR PARENTING. THE BIBLE DOESN'T GIVE DETAILED STRATEGIES, BUT THERE ARE AMPLE PRINCIPLES. WHAT PRINCIPLES HAVE YOU LEARNED IN THESE PASSAGES AND OTHERS IN THE BIBLE THAT YOU CAN APPLY TO YOUR PARENTING?

2. WHAT IS THE GOSPEL-INFORMED AIM OF PARENTING? (HINT: THE GOAL OF CHRISTIAN PARENTING IS NOT SIMPLY CONVERSION!)

3. WHAT ARE YOUR RESPONSIBILITIES AS AN AMBASSADOR OF CHRIST IN YOUR HOME?

*Our anxiety over the unknown reveals
an issue in our hearts.*

The Gospel for Seasons of Waiting

READ: PSALM 62:5-8, ISAIAH 54:1-8, HEBREWS 11

Begin by carefully reading today's Scripture passages before coming back to this page. As you read through the passages, focus on how they speak to the seasons of waiting that we may experience in our lives.

Waiting is hard. Whether you are waiting on a spouse, a baby, a job, or any number of other things, the passing time can be agonizing and, in many cases, heartbreaking. But take heart; the gospel offers hope for the waiting.

Waiting wouldn't be so hard if we knew what the outcome would be and when it would happen. We wouldn't be so anxious about paying rent if we knew God was going to give us the money the day before it is due. We wouldn't mind waiting on a spouse if we knew we would meet sometime within the next year. We wouldn't be so worried about the present if we could see the future. Our anxiety over the unknown reveals an issue in our hearts; We don't believe God. God says He is good, He is in control, and He is for us (Psalm 107:1, Psalm 115:3, Romans 8:31-32). Because of the gospel, we who were once enemies of God are now children of God, and His eternal power that was once against us in wrath is now for us in love. If we believe He is who He says He is, we can trust fully in His timing and His outcome, knowing that the God who knows all things can and will do what is best for us. We may be anxious over uncertainty, but God is never anxious because nothing is uncertain to Him. We can rest in the unknown because it is not unknown to God.

We are impatient people, and when we do not quickly see answers or results, our tendency is to rush to fears that God has forgotten us or forsaken us. We see waiting as the enemy, but there is beauty in waiting. God promised Israel a Messiah, a King who would rescue them from sin and death. From the first veiled promise of a Savior to come in Genesis 3:15 until the Son of God was born in Bethlehem, God's people would experience slavery, famine, and war, ending in an agonizing 400 years of waiting while God seemed silent. But God's people also experienced something else in their long season of waiting—God's faithfulness. In ways they could see and ways they could not, God was working to set everything perfectly into place so that only when the timing was perfect would He send the Messiah (Galatians 4:4-5), strengthening their faith in the process. Just as God sent Christ in the fullness of time, God will work in your life in the way and in the timing that is perfect. From our perspective, God may seem to be moving too slowly to act on our behalf, but our view of slow is not slow in God's eyes. He will not delay His promise (2 Peter 2:9). He works in His timing, and His timing is perfect.

What about those of us who never obtain the thing we were waiting for? What happens to your faith when you don't find a spouse, or you are unable to conceive a child? Is God unfaithful? Sometimes we do not receive the things we wait for in this life, but the good news of the gospel is that though we experience brokenness in this sin-ridden world, Christ will return and make all things right. Like those in Hebrews 11 who lived by faith but did not see the fulfillment of the promise before they died, we have hope in the truth that because of the gospel, this world is not our home. Even if we do not see answers to our waiting in this life, we know with confidence that we will experience the fulfillment of every promise when Christ returns. Even if we do not find the spouse we long for in this life, Christ, our perfect groom, is coming for us. Even if we experience the heartbreak of an empty womb, we will live eternally with the spiritual children that we have discipled in this lifetime as one body of Christ. Every longing of our hearts, every unmet expectation, every question, all of it will be met in Christ.

We wait expectantly for the revealing of our hope and salvation when Christ returns, rejoicing in the promise we glimpse from afar. We still feel the bitter sting of disappointment and longing in this lifetime, so what do we do with that pain? We join the Psalmist in pouring out our hearts before God—our rock, our refuge, our fortress. When our hearts are restless with uncertainty and confusion, we can rest in the mighty arms of our loving Father. When we feel as if we are crumbling under the weight of fear, God is our strong rock that holds us up when we cannot stand on our own. When we feel vulnerable and alone in our longing, God covers us and protects us. He is a safe place. God does not leave us alone in our waiting, but He invites us to pour out all our hopes, joys, sorrows, and fears before Him, and promises that even when all seems hopeless, He will guard our hearts with a peace that endures despite our circumstances, the peace that comes from the one who knows all and holds all (Philippians 4:6-7).

We might not know what tomorrow holds, but we do know the future. We do not know how He will fulfill His promises, but we do know that they will be fulfilled. We do not know how God will answer the longings of our heart, but we do know that the answer will result in our eternal joy. God is with us in the waiting, and He will be with us when the waiting is over.

God does not leave us alone in our waiting, but He invites us to pour out all our hopes, joys, sorrows, and fears before Him.

1. WHAT ARE YOU CURRENTLY WAITING FOR? WHAT DOES YOUR RESPONSE TO WAITING REVEAL ABOUT WHAT YOU BELIEVE TO BE TRUE OF GOD?

2. HOW DOES THE FUTURE PROMISE OF THE GOSPEL GIVE YOU HOPE IN THE WAITING?

3. READ PHILIPPIANS 4:6-7. WRITE A PRAYER PRESENTING YOUR REQUESTS TO GOD IN THE WAITING.

So, whether you eat or drink, or whatever you do, do everything for the glory of God.

I CORINTHIANS 10:31

PARAPHRASE THE PASSAGES FROM THIS WEEK.

_____

_____

_____

_____

_____

_____

_____

_____

_____

_____

WHAT DID YOU OBSERVE FROM THIS WEEK'S TEXT ABOUT
GOD AND HIS CHARACTER?

_____

_____

_____

_____

_____

WHAT DO THESE PASSAGES TEACH ABOUT THE CONDITION OF
MANKIND AND ABOUT YOURSELF?

_____

_____

_____

_____

_____

_____

HOW DO THESE PASSAGES POINT TO THE GOSPEL?

HOW SHOULD YOU RESPOND TO THESE PASSAGES?
WHAT IS THE PERSONAL APPLICATION?

WHAT SPECIFIC ACTION STEPS CAN YOU TAKE THIS WEEK
TO APPLY THESE PASSAGES?

*We are called to love our neighbors and
to pursue the love of strangers.*

The Gospel and Hospitality

READ: LEVITICUS 19:33-34, ROMANS 12:9-21, LUKE 10:25-37

Begin by carefully reading today's Scripture passages. As you read through the passages, focus on how the gospel informs our relationships with others.

Hospitality—when you hear that word, what image comes to mind? Is it a farmhouse table beautifully set with perfectly hand-lettered seat cards, chargers under vintage plates, and gourmet food? Or maybe it's perfectly puffed up couch pillows and a deep-cleaned hallway bathroom. Or maybe we think of the hospitality industry—hotels that offer room service and crisp white linens. Essentially, when we think of hospitality, we think of inviting others into a space to entertain them. We may consider it a noble endeavor that requires a lot of prep work—like cleaning the house from top to bottom and preparing a delicious meal. But does it really require that much forethought and staging? Or is it simply having an open home motivated by an open heart?

The word for hospitality in Greek is *philoxenia*. Its root words are *philos* and *zenos*, which are friend and stranger, respectively. Put together, hospitality simply means love of strangers—a stranger being anyone who is not you. In the Bible, hospitality is a love for stranger that is expressed in meeting his or her physical and spiritual needs. It is considered a required virtue of elders (Titus 1:8), but all believers are told to "seek to show hospitality" (Romans 12:13). But what does biblical hospitality entail? Why is it so highly esteemed in the Word of God?

Biblical hospitality is focused on others, not self. It is focused on meeting others' needs, not invoking self-admiration. It strives to refresh others, not impress them. It is not cost-dependent—an immaculate home, gourmet food, and fancy table settings are not required. It is not entertainment. Hospitality is commanded throughout Scripture because the purpose of extending hospitality is to tangibly show the gospel to others. It is welcoming, befriending, and loving others because we have been welcomed, befriended, and loved by Christ. It is a humble character trait that adorns His people because, ultimately, it is the reverence of God being reflected in the life of a believer. Love for neighbor is an act of obedience motivated by the love of God.

We are called to love our neighbors and to pursue the love of strangers (Mark 12:31, Romans 12:13). But who are our neighbors? Are they to be differentiated from the strangers that we encounter? In Luke 10:29, we see a lawyer ask Jesus, "Who is my neighbor?" He asked this question because he wanted to know what was required to inherit eternal life. After some exchange, Jesus shared the parable of the Good Samaritan. In this parable, the Samaritan acted as a neighbor to a stranger. He saw the man's needs, not his ethnicity, and met them. Jesus was using this parable to teach His followers to ask the better question of "Who am I?" Ultimately, both of the lawyer's questions hinge on identity—who are you? Our eternal security relies on our union with Christ. And our union with Christ informs the way we see those around us. Because of Christ, we see others as image bearers of our Creator in need of the gospel. Our encounters are seen as opportunities to be who we are in Christ. By the indwelling Holy Spirit, we are empowered to love others—neighbors and strangers—as Christ does. The Apostle Peter says to "be hospitable to one another without complaining"—a state of being that is characterized by joy, imitating our God that is hospitable and gracious toward us (1 Peter 4:9).

This is how biblical hospitality is a vehicle of evangelism. It is a way of living that proclaims the gospel. As we share our lives, we share the gospel because our lives are living epistles. As biblical hospitality seeks to meet the physical and spiritual needs of others, we understand that the greatest need of every single person is the need for Christ. This is why the gospel is what informs the practical implications of biblical hospitality—what can I do to serve someone else to show them the love, hope, and glorious reality of Christ?

And that's where we start on this journey—look around and identify who God has placed in your vicinity. If you are married, your husband is your neighbor and should be the re-cipient of your hospitality. If you have kids, your children are your neighbors, too. Where do you frequent regularly? Who also frequents those places? This could be your workplace, the grocery store, the gym, or the bus stop. Or maybe it's the waiting room at your child's therapy or the school pick-up line. What needs do you see in those people? What are good questions that will help you identify others' needs? Then, intentionally utilize your gifts to meet those needs. Maybe you are a great cook and can offer a refreshing meal in your home. Maybe you're a talented mechanic and can help with the broken lawn mower. Maybe you're in a season of little ones—opening your heart and your home may look like inviting someone in a similar season to join you in your backyard with a cup of coffee.

Opening your heart and your home is an act of obedience motivated by love for the Father. It is choosing to see others as image bearers with intrinsic worth given to them by the Creator, no matter how different they are from you. It is using what was freely given to you to generously meet the needs of others. It is making God's compassion known to others by extending compassion in the name of Jesus. It may be risky and uncomfortable. It will require vulnerability. It may even be costly in terms of your time and finances. But it will be worth it because He's worthy. Biblical hospitality is not just offering soup and bread or some sort of service. It's offering the bread of life and the humble Servant that laid down His life as a ransom for many (John 6:35, Mark 10:45).

1. BASED ON TODAY'S PASSAGES, WHO ARE YOU? WHO ARE YOUR NEIGHBORS?

2. WHAT IS BIBLICAL HOSPITALITY? HOW DOES IT DIFFER FROM WHAT THE WORLD PROMOTES AS HOSPITALITY?

3. TO WHOM CAN YOU SHOW BIBLICAL HOSPITALITY? TAKE SOME TIME TO WRITE SPECIFIC ACTION STEPS TO SHOW THEM BIBLICAL HOSPITALITY THIS WEEK.

Christ died to redeem the Church, and to be a part of this glorious body is grace upon grace.

The Gospel and The Local Church

READ: EPHESIANS 2:19-22, EPHESIANS 4:11-16, EPHESIANS 5:22-32, ROMANS 12:3-8, HEBREWS 10:19-25, I CORINTHIANS 12:12-27

Begin by carefully reading today's Scripture passages before returning to this page. As you read, focus on God's definition of and purpose for the Church.

When you hear the word church, what comes to mind? Perhaps you think of stained glass windows and kneelers. Maybe you picture a group of twenty-somethings in t-shirts and jeans singing and sipping coffee. Or maybe you cringe at the mention of church, remembering hurt and pain that prevents you from ever wanting to step foot inside a church again. Whether your understanding of church aligns with one of these examples or is totally different, the gospel gives a picture of the Church that is very different from the ways that most of us understand it.

When we talk about the universal church, we are referring to the collective people of God who have been saved by grace through faith. The church is not a physical building, but a spiritual one, made up of all those who have been transformed by the gospel, whether currently living on earth or not, and are being built up together into the dwelling place of the Holy Spirit (Ephesians 2:22, 1 Peter 2:5). Scripture frequently describes the church as the body and bride of Christ. The gospel is not just that Christ saves individuals, but that He redeems the Church, sanctifying her so that she can be presented to Him as His pure and holy bride. We look forward to the day when Christ returns and we, His bride, will be united to Him in total sinlessness and purity. The good news of our union with Christ also means union with all those who are united to Him — His body, His bride, His church.

We are not saved into isolation, but into community. The corporate nature of our union with Christ has huge implications for the way we live in relationship to one another in the local church. While the universal Church consists of all believers and our common union with Christ, the local church refers to an organized gathering of believers who live, worship, and serve in community with one another. We tend to view the purpose of the local church as a place for believers to be fed and grow in faith as we receive encouragement through the preaching of God's Word. This understanding of church is not entirely incorrect, but it is incomplete. This individualistic view of the local church leads us to believe that we can get just as much, if not more, out of live-streaming a sermon in our pajamas as we can from consistently and physically attending a corporate worship service. But this is not God's design for His people.

In light of the truth of the gospel, the author of Hebrews calls us to draw near to God in full assurance of faith to which we hold firmly with one another. We are not to neglect the gathering of God's people, but join together to encourage one another as we spur each other on to holiness. God is concerned not only with the sanctification of the individual, but of the whole body, of which we are individually members (Romans 12:5). This kind of growth does not happen from your couch through a computer screen. This kind of growth requires authentic relationships between members of the body where we can be encouraged and challenged to grow, it requires submission to church leadership who have been established by God to encourage, correct, and rebuke us for our protection so that we will hold fast to the truth and not be led astray by destructive teaching (2 Timothy 4:2-4). When we join together for a worship service, sing the truth of God's Word over one another, and experience the Lord's Supper and baptism together, we grow together.

We are called not only to individual growth, but to grow up into Christ as one body. We need each other. We can't function properly without one another. Just like all the different parts of our bodies have different functions, so every member of the body of Christ has been created with different gifts and abilities for the purpose of the mutual sanctification of the whole. A foot cannot work apart from the rest of the body, and a body without a foot cannot function in the capacity in which it was created to function. So it is with the body of Christ. No matter your gift, God is calling you to use it for the good of your brothers and sisters in Christ, and this happens primarily within the context of the local church.

Are you gifted to teach? God calls you to teach His Word for the good of the body. Do you love to cook? You can bless those who are struggling with difficult seasons with a meal. Consider how you might offer hospitality to someone in your church who is between jobs. All of our resources and abilities are gifts from God, and we are called to use them for the building up of the body. Whether we watch a sermon online, sit through Sunday services without connecting with the members of the body, or have no involvement in a local church at all, we are being disobedient to God's commands if we are not actively serving and participating in a local church. In our individualistic mindsets, we tend to think of church only in the context of how it benefits us and how it helps us grow in our own faith, but if we are not actively participating in the local church, we are not only shortchanging ourselves, but we are shortchanging our brothers and sisters in Christ.

Christ died to redeem the Church, and to be a part of this glorious body is grace upon grace. Let us joyfully serve and participate in the local expression of the universal church as we grow in love and holiness into Christ.

1. HOW DOES THE GOSPEL INFORM YOUR UNDERSTANDING OF THE LOCAL CHURCH?

2. WHAT DO THE FOLLOWING IMAGES FOR THE CHURCH REVEAL ABOUT THE IMPORTANCE OF THE LOCAL CHURCH?

BUILDING	BRIDE	BODY

3. WHAT ABILITIES OR RESOURCES HAS GOD GIVEN YOU? HOW CAN YOU PRACTICALLY USE THEM TO SERVE THE MEMBERS OF THE BODY?

We are called to live in community with other believers in the context of the local church.

The Gospel and Community

READ: MARK 12:28-34, JOHN 15:1-22

Begin by carefully reading today's Scripture passages. As you read through the passages, focus on how the gospel and our union with Christ compels us to love others.

One aspect of the church is community. There are a variety of different communities in our culture today, and most are essentially similar interest groups. People are apart of a number of different tribes. So what are we talking about in regard to the word community? For believers, this is two-fold. It begins with our community within the body of Christ, and then extends to the greater community of the world. Meaningful engagement with both communities are necessary, but there is a noteworthy distinction between the two.

A mark of a healthy church is church membership because membership denotes commitment to the body. This commitment is expressed in consistent presence, faithful prayer, and generous service to one another. As believers, we are called to live in community with other believers in the context of the local church. And the church is composed of diverse people that are united by Christ. Is it not a remarkable testament of our God when people that are so incredibly different from one another are gathered together? The work Christ does in our hearts to transform us permeates to the way we interact with others and causes us to live in community with those that a seemingly vastly different from

us. This kind of work that the Spirit does in us causes the world to look in disbelief. It goes against the ethnocentric tendency deeply embedded in human nature. The church's unity and diversity that are achieved by the blood of Christ and the power of the Holy Spirit reflects the Trinity because in the Trinity, we see perfect unity between the three persons that are distinct in their roles.

But as believers, we are called to embrace God's commitment to see His glory spread throughout the earth. We first see it in God's command to Adam and Eve before the Fall to "be fruitful and multiply and fill the earth" (Genesis 1:28). We see it after the Fall when God commands Noah to do the same. And then again in the Abrahamic covenant where "all the families" will be included through the work of Christ. From Genesis to Revelation, we see that God has a global purpose to save His people—a people that will be from "every nation, from all tribes and peoples and languages" (Revelation 7:9). As a community of believers, we are called to join Him in that global mission. In essence, our community within the local church is called to engage the greater community of the world. This global mission is not reserved for specific individuals that feel the unique call to serve the unreached peoples of the world. No, it is a calling for each of us and it begins in our immediate communities.

We are called to proclaim the good news to all people, and we can begin right where we are in our respective communities. But how do we proclaim the good news? Is it being well-versed in certain methodologies, like the Romans Road? Or is there a more organic approach? It is important to remember that "faith comes from hearing, and hearing through the word of Christ" (Romans 10:17). The word of Christ is the message about Christ — the gospel. The power is in the Word of God — the gospel of Jesus Christ — not in our perfectly curated presentations. Words are necessary. Looking at Jesus' public ministry, it was clear that preaching was His primary goal. Healing the sick and casting out demons were secondary. News spreads through words not actions. In the same way, we share the gospel in words.

However, we can show the gospel through our deeds. Believers are image bearers that have transformed hearts because of God's irresistible pursuit. Because of Him, we are branches that are grafted into the true vine, Jesus (John 15:1). He is our life source. And this metaphor of the vine and branches in John 15 makes it easy to see that the purpose of the branch is to bear good fruit, and its ability to do so is wholly due to its connection to the vine. Jesus said, "as the branch cannot bear fruit by itself, unless it abides in the vine, neither can you, unless you abide in me." He then makes it clear that in order to abide in His love, we must keep His commandments. Naturally, we remember what Jesus said are the two most important commandments:

The most important is Listen, O Israel! The Lord our God, the Lord is one. Love the Lord your God with all your heart, with all your soul, with all your mind, and with all your strength. The second is, Love your neighbor as yourself. There is no other command greater than these. (Mark 12:29-31)

We are called to love God and love others. Our love for God will manifest in our lives — in our words, thoughts, and deeds. And it is our love for God that will compel us to love others. When we consider our engagement with our community, we must keep this order in mind.

What does it mean to love our neighbors as ourselves? It begins by agreeing with Scripture that our neighbors are image bearers of God. All humans are equal in worth and dignity. It is also recognizing that the essence of sin is self-exaltation. God's perfect design puts self after God and others. It's a battle between flesh and the Spirit. But we are empowered by the Holy Spirit to see our neighbors as God sees them and to crucify the flesh "with its passions and desires" (Galatians 5:24). And when we do, our lives look radically countercultural and the only explanation is the gospel.

The practical implications are endless. Though there are godly attributes that characterize believers, there is not a specific formula or a holy to-do list that is implied by the command to love our neighbors as ourselves. Our respective communities have various needs that we are equipped by the grace of God to meet. A helpful starting point is to consider what daily needs that we meet for ourselves. Every day, we expend energy in making sure that we are appropriately clothed and adequately fed. We engage our minds and hearts in conversations with those that care to listen and reciprocate. Are there those in our community that don't have their basic needs met? Do they need somewhere to sleep, food to eat, or clothes to match the season and therefore, protect their dignity? Do they feel seen and treated as an image bearer of God? Our world is experiencing a loneliness epidemic by both those in the outskirts of our society and those in the very center. Are we willing to do the hard work of identifying needs that cannot be assessed at a glance? Are we willing to establish relationships across the social, ethnic, and economic strata for the sake of the gospel? Are we willing to intentionally seek ways where our unique gifts can be used for the glory of God?

We engage our communities in love and obedience to our Lord. We are motivated by Jesus, the greatest need of every image bearer.

He is the One that offers the forgiveness of sins and the righteousness that God's just wrath demands. Our lives are marked by kindness and generosity to show the gospel so that we can share the gospel in clear words that come from the Word of God. We start in our immediate communities, but we don't stop there. We keep God's global purpose in mind and join Him in His mission.

1. BASED ON TODAY'S PASSAGES, HOW IS OUR LOVE FOR GOD CONNECTED TO OUR LOVE FOR OUR NEIGHBORS, LOCALLY AND GLOBALLY?

2. SPEND SOME TIME THINKING AND PRAYING OVER YOUR IMMEDIATE COMMUNITY. WHAT TANGIBLE NEEDS CAN YOU IDENTIFY THAT YOU AND YOUR FAMILY CAN WORK TO MEET?

3. GOOD DEEDS CAN BE USED TO SHOW THE GOSPEL, BUT WORDS ARE NEEDED TO SHARE THE GOSPEL. THERE IS POWER IN THE WORD OF GOD. WHO CAN YOU SHARE THE GOSPEL WITH? WRITE OUT WHAT YOU WOULD SAY.

As members of His body, we are not only united to Him, but also to one another.

The Gospel and Friendship

READ: ROMANS 12:9-18, EPHESIANS 4:25-32, PHILIPPIANS 2:1-11, COLOSSIANS 3:1-17

Begin by carefully reading today's Scripture passages before coming back to this page. As you read through the passages, focus on how the gospel transforms friendship and how Christ is a model of true friendship.

Everyone longs for friendship. We all want people we can have fun with, people who can love and encourage us, and people to call when we have a bad day. Our desire for this kind of companionship is part of God's design. All believers are united to Christ, not only as individuals, but as members of a larger whole, the church, which is Christ's body. As members of His body, we are not only united to Him, but also to one another. This supernatural union means that friendships among believers should look radically different from the type of friendship that the world pursues.

One of the major ways that biblical friendship differs from the world's view of friendship is that for believers, friendship has the goal of helping one another grow in holiness. The gospel calls us to sanctification, but it does not call us to grow alone. As members of one another, we are called to mature together into the likeness of Christ, a process that will be stunted without other members of the body. In Ephesians 4, Paul gives a picture of what this kind of mutual sanctification looks like practically. Friends ought to speak the truth to our brothers and sisters in Christ, not out of anger, but in love. Typically, if an issue arises where a friend is behaving in a way that is detrimental to themselves or to someone else, our temptation is to either ignore the problem in the name of acceptance and non-judgment, or to react out of a place of anger against our friend. But the believer is called to something higher and far more difficult. We are called to confront sin in the lives of our believing friends, not to condemn them, but in order to bring them back to the truth of the gospel and away from the path of death that they are treading (James 5:19-20). Not only that, but we are to be humbly receptive to the correction of our friends, not defensive or hostile, knowing that a friend's rebuke is trustworthy and should cause us to grow in knowledge and in holiness (Proverbs 26:7, Proverbs 19:25).

Ephesians 4 also paints a picture of Christian friendships that should be marked not by harsh words and slander that come from bitterness and anger, but by kind, compassionate, and encouraging speech. Instead of basing our interactions with our friends on what we feel or desire, we are to act in response to the question, "How can I meet the needs of my friend with grace?" Offering grace to our friends means pointing them back to the gospel of grace. Sometimes this looks like a well timed word of encouragement, and sometimes it looks like calling out the sin in their lives, the fruit of which is not life, but death (Romans 6:21). Knowing what is appropriate requires wisdom and discernment from the Holy Spirit who directs our hearts to act not out of prideful malice but out of humble love.

Humility is a vital ingredient in biblical friendship. Philippians 2 gives us a model of what it means to be humble in our relationships with one another, giving Christ as the ultimate example of humble love. Humble love does not seek to be above one other, but strives for unity as members of one body, putting aside competition and instead lowering ourselves below our friends. We are so quick to approach friendship selfishly, focusing on how we can benefit from the relationship, but we are called to think first about how we can serve our friends, counting their needs as more important than our own. We practice this kind of self-sacrificial love because it is what Christ did for us. If there was anyone who deserved to be served, it was Jesus Christ, the perfect, sinless, Son of God. He was entitled to all glory and riches, but He willingly laid it all down—laid himself down—lower than us, wretches that we were, counting the lives of sinners as more valuable than His own. Christ's own sacrifice compels and empowers us to humble ourselves as we seek the good of our friends.

When we consider that Christ gave His very life for our brothers and sisters in Christ, that reality ought to give real weight to the way we treat our friends. It is our general tendency to walk away from relationships when they become difficult. A friend hurts us or disagrees with us, and we cut them out of our lives. We follow the exhortations of our culture to get rid of anyone in your life who is not making you happy and trash-talking them to anyone who will listen. This mindset is like being frustrated that your check engine light keeps coming on and choosing to forego repair costs and get rid of the engine all together. The car cannot function without the engine, and neither can we say "I have no need of you" to a fellow member of the body of Christ (1 Corinthians 12:21). As believers, we should fight for our friendships, knowing that Christ gave His very life that we might be united to one another as we are united to Him. This doesn't mean our relationships will be without conflict, but that we respond to conflict with forgiveness, running hard after peace and reconciliation (Psalm 34:14). In our sin nature, we seek our own honor, respond to criticism defensively, and try to be first, but as believers we are called not to outdo one another in prestige, but in showing honor to the other. The only competition we should have as believers is who can love the most.

Friendships among believers should be marked by a sweetness that is impossible apart from Christ. We are united to each other, sanctified together, and ultimately glorified together as the pure bride of Christ. We have the joy that comes from our mutual hope in Christ, a hope that we will rejoice in together for eternity, and we link arms in the cause of the spread of the gospel so that others might join into this sweet friendship in Christ. Let us be for one another as God is for us.

1. HOW DOES YOUR UNION WITH CHRIST AND YOUR UNION WITH OTHER BELIEVERS CHANGE THE WAY YOU VIEW FRIENDSHIP?

2. WHAT ARE SOME CHARACTERISTICS OF THE WORLD'S IDEA OF FRIENDSHIP AND OF THE BIBLICAL VIEW OF FRIENDSHIP AS DESCRIBED IN TODAY'S READINGS?

WORLDY FRIENDSHIP	BIBLICAL FRIENDSHIP

3. HOW WAS CHRIST THE MODEL OF TRUE FRIENDSHIP? WHAT PRACTICAL STEPS CAN YOU TAKE TO IMITATE HIS EXAMPLE IN YOUR OWN FRIENDSHIPS?

Our daily work can be done in service and worship to God by serving others.

The Gospel and Work

READ: 1 CORINTHIANS 7:17-24, 2 THESSALONIANS 3:6-15

Begin by carefully reading today's Scripture passages. As you read through the passages, focus on the implications of the gospel on our work on this side of eternity.

The root of the word vocation comes from the Latin word *vocare*, which means to call. This projects the sense that one's vocation is a calling—someone has given the call to another to do something, and in response, work is completed for the one that gave the calling. It is obvious that the majority of people do not see their jobs in this way. Instead, many people work simply out of necessity. Others genuinely enjoy their work. It gives them a sense of fulfillment. But what does the Bible have to say about work? Is there instruction for a believer in a secular workplace? What if the work is in the home? How does the gospel inform the relationship between faith and work?

Work appears in the very first pages of the Bible. God created the heavens and the earth in a regular work week. Then He commissioned Adam and Eve to "fill the earth and subdue it" (Genesis 1:28). They were to cultivate the land in such a way as to yield riches according to God's design with the goal of accomplishing His purposes. This means that work is not a result of sin; work is actually deemed good. Jesus said in John 5:17, "My Father is still working, and I am working also." As His image bearers, it is in our design to work. However, it is also in God's design for us to rest. He has given us God-ordained limits that require rest. This serves as a reminder that work is not our ultimate purpose in this life—it is a gift from God that can be a means to worship Him.

In our union with Christ, there is freedom and this freedom transcends our job descriptions. The Apostle Paul writes in 1 Corinthians 7:17, "Let each one live his life in the situation the Lord assigned when God called him." God is the One that does the bidding. He pursues us in our salvation and in the working out of our salvation, which simply refers to our continual obedience and partnership with the Holy Spirit in our sanctification. God is the One who has ordained our salvation and good works before the foundation of the world. But how do we navigate the reality of hard work in and out of the workforce today?

First, we must remember that our work, whatever it may be, is a calling from God. God's callings are not limited to church ministries but extend to secular jobs. The gospel clearly tells us that we are justified by grace through faith in Jesus—it is a free gift from God, wholly independent of our works (Ephesians 2:8-9). Thus, right standing before God is irrespective of the work of a full-time pastor versus the work of a full-time dental hygienist. God, in His glorious plan, equips individuals with gifts and abilities that are used to excel in a variety of vocations. However, if we view our work as a calling, we are saying that it is an assignment given by God that should be completed for Him. And in the Bible, we see that our daily work can be done in service and worship to God by serving others. So the better question to ask is, "How can my gifts and abilities, in light of the opportunities before me, be used to best serve others and bring glory to God?"

This transforms work from being an exhausting duty to a gifted means to express our love for God and neighbor. The underlying purpose of all work is to honor God by loving our neighbors through service. However, work is hard. After the fall, work came under the curse of sin. We know this intimately because we experience it, whether we work inside or outside of the home. In our work, we come face to face with the brokenness of the world and the sinfulness of our flesh. Our efforts don't always translate into success. Our gifts and abilities may not align with the opportunities in front of us. We experience conflict in our workplaces because we are sinful humans working alongside other sinful humans. Opportunities for frustration abound. Our jobs may also be avenues in which we misplace our identities or engage in idolatry.

This is when we need the gospel. The gospel reminds us of God's good purpose for our work. The gospel reminds us that this purpose beckons an outward focus to serve God and neighbor rather than ourselves. This is how our faith sets apart our work, and in turn, how our work can be a means to sanctify us and grow our faith. With a gospel-informed purpose and focus, we are less likely to wrestle with burn-out and frustration and disenchantment. The gospel reminds us that, as believers, our true identity is rooted in the person and work of Christ alone. In Christ we are saints, recipients of His grace, redeemed, dead to sin, eternally alive, and more. And as new creations, we are invited to participate in His work on this side of eternity in a variety of capacities, knowing that He is continually at work even now in His work of redemption, providence, and more. Whether our vocation is CEO of a large corporation yielding a six-figure salary or CEO of our household with no monetary compensation, our efforts have kingdom value when they are done for the glory of God. We can work with diligence and excellence "as for the Lord not for men" and fight against idleness (Colossians 3:23).

God's callings are not limited to church ministries but extend to secular jobs.

1. BASED ON TODAY'S PASSAGES, TO WHAT REGARD DOES GOD CONSIDER OUR WORK ON THIS SIDE OF ETERNITY? WHY DOES THAT MATTER?

2. WHAT ARE THE IMPLICATIONS IN CONSIDERING YOUR WORK INSIDE OR OUTSIDE OF THE HOME, WITH OR WITHOUT MONETARY COMPENSATION AS A CALLING FROM GOD?

3. WHAT ARE THE EFFECTS OF OUR WORK COMING UNDER THE CURSE OF SIN? HOW DOES THE GOSPEL REDEEM OUR WORK?

By this everyone will know that you are my disciples, if you love one another.

JOHN 13:35

PARAPHRASE THE PASSAGES FROM THIS WEEK.

_____
_____
_____
_____
_____
_____
_____
_____
_____

WHAT DID YOU OBSERVE FROM THIS WEEK'S TEXT ABOUT
GOD AND HIS CHARACTER?

_____
_____
_____
_____
_____

WHAT DO THESE PASSAGES TEACH ABOUT THE CONDITION OF
MANKIND AND ABOUT YOURSELF?

_____
_____
_____
_____
_____
_____
_____

HOW DO THESE PASSAGES POINT TO THE GOSPEL?

HOW SHOULD YOU RESPOND TO THESE PASSAGES?
WHAT IS THE PERSONAL APPLICATION?

WHAT SPECIFIC ACTION STEPS CAN YOU TAKE THIS WEEK
TO APPLY THESE PASSAGES?

*By His grace we experience Him
every moment of every day.*

The Gospel and Free Time

READ: I CORINTHIANS 10:31, COLOSSIANS 3:12-17, I TIMOTHY 6:17-19, I TIMOTHY 4:1-5 , PSALM 19

Begin by carefully reading today's Scripture passages before coming back to this page. As you read through the passages, consider how they influence the way we think about our free time.

Does what we do in our free time matter? What difference does it make if we decide to read a book, get coffee with a friend, or play a pickup basketball game? Is it a waste of time to do things for fun when we could be studying Scripture or serving our neighbors? Perhaps you have never considered how Christ should impact the things you do for fun, but the gospel applies even to this area of our lives.

It can be our tendency to compartmentalize our lives. Work, play, time with God—all of these have a place in our lives with time specifically dedicated to each. But God's Word rejects the sacred-secular divide that we create. Through the gospel the whole of our lives have been redeemed for God's glory. God commands us to live all of life as worship to the glory of God. This command means that we don't just encounter God for thirty minutes in the morning while we read the Bible, but by His grace we experience Him every moment of every day. Just as we can work to the glory of God, we can also play to the glory of God.

We do not have a God who requires joyless obedience or dutiful monotony, but we have a God who calls us to delight. As believers, our lives should not be less fun than the rest of the world, but abundantly more enjoyable and fulfilling as we delight in our good God through the good gifts that He gives us. Everything that God created is good and is for our enjoyment—from food, to music, to crisp fall afternoons—all of it is meant to point us to the greater joy found in Him. When we listen to beautiful music, it ought to move our hearts to marvel at the One who composes all of history into a glorious symphony with all of its parts working together in perfect harmony. When we eat a delicious dessert, we should rejoice in the knowledge that His Words are even sweeter. When we see a movie that we love, we can see how it reflects the story of redemption and how the story He is writing is far greater than superheroes or fairy tales.

Think about the photographs you have in your home. The faces of family or friends are placed strategically on bedside tables or living room walls. Why do we smile when we see these images? The pictures may have a certain degree of beauty in themselves, but the photograph is not the true object of our delight, the person in the picture is the object. No matter how beautifully photographed a portrait is, we will never delight in a picture of a total stranger in the same way we delight in a picture of a son or daughter or friend. So is it with the gifts God has created for our enjoyment. If we look to the things that God has made without knowing the creator Himself, we will delight only in the creature, and so idolize it. But if we have tasted the goodness of God, if we have delighted in His character, then our joy in experiencing creation will be exponentially greater because our true delight is in God Himself. As we experience the goodness of creation, the beauty we behold calls to mind the superior glory of the creator to whom it points.

In addition to worshiping God through delighting in His works, we can also use our hobbies to glorify God by displaying His character as image bearers. Many hobbies are in some sense creative, and can display the superior creative nature of God. Whether you play an instrument, cook meals, write, paint, or organize and decorate your home, all people can reflect God's image through creativity. While our creativity is simply rearranging what God has already made, God creates from nothing, speaking matter and life into existence and adorning it with beauty.

When we enjoy what God has made for our enjoyment, our gaze can become idolatry as we fixate on the gift or in worship as we stand in awe of the Creator. When we decide how we will play, we ought to examine our own hearts and prayerfully ask ourselves three questions:

1. *How can this activity serve to increase my delight in the Lord?*

2. *How can I glorify God through this activity?*

3. *How can I love my neighbor through this activity?*

We can participate in identical activities and approach them from a totally different heart. Doing everything in the name of Christ and for the glory of God requires actively orienting our minds and hearts toward God. If we cannot truthfully answer these questions, we may want to reconsider how we are choosing to spend our time. In Christ we can fulfill all three of those questions in things like enjoying good food, friendship, movies, softball, and so on, but not when our actions are done in sin.

To truly enjoy God's gifts in their proper place, we must have a greater affection for God Himself. The primary way that this affection is cultivated is through the Word of God. In Scripture God reveals who He is, and we glimpse the glory of our holy God in its pages. God's glory is put on display in the gospel, perfectly radiating through Jesus Christ (Hebrews 1:3). As we return continually to God's Word, our love and affection for Him grows, and our enjoyment of all of the pleasures of life is enhanced and put into proper perspective.

1. HOW SHOULD THE GOSPEL IMPACT THE WAY WE VIEW OUR FREE TIME?

2. HOW DOES KNOWING AND DELIGHTING IN GOD THROUGH HIS WORD IMPACT THE WAY WE ENJOY HIS GIFTS?

3. CONSIDER AN ACTIVITY YOU LIKE TO DO IN YOUR FREE TIME AND ANSWER THE THREE QUESTIONS PREVIOUSLY MENTIONED: HOW CAN THIS ACTIVITY SERVE TO INCREASE MY DELIGHT IN THE LORD? HOW CAN I GLORIFY GOD THROUGH THIS ACTIVITY? HOW CAN I LOVE MY NEIGHBOR THROUGH THIS ACTIVITY

*Our treasures reveal the
loves of our hearts.*

The Gospel and Resources

READ: ROMANS 13:1-7, MATTHEW 6:19-24, 2 CORINTHIANS 9:6-7, GALATIANS 6:7-10

Begin by carefully reading today's Scripture passages before coming back to this page. As you read through the passages, consider what it means to sow and reap in regard to our resources, and how the gospel informs our manner of sowing.

The topic of money is one that most people inside and outside of the church avoid. How much we have in our possession and the manner in which we spend it seem incredibly personal. We are highly resistant to anyone advising us on how to manage our resources. Nonetheless, how we spend our time and money are actually good barometers for our spirituality. This is because our bank statements and our calendars are concrete indicators of our values and priorities. And we cannot ignore the fact that the Word of God has a lot to say about money. This is because all of our resources are really about the stewardship of our lives.

Earlier in this study, we learned that being a steward is someone that is entrusted with someone else's resources, and they are responsible for whatever is given to them. This is absolutely true with our resources. Our time and money are His. Psalm 24:1 says it clearly, "The earth and everything in it, the world and its inhabitants, belong to the Lord." And though the blood of Christ covers believers, the Bible also tells us that "each of us will give an account of himself to God" (Romans 14:12). This is what stewards do. They tell the owners exactly how they managed the resources entrusted to them. This is why it's imperative that we have a biblical perspective on our possessions and live in line with the principles given to us in the Word of God.

We faithfully give to the local church and other organizations (seminaries, missionaries, etc.) to support, ultimately, the spread of the gospel for the glory of God. A common passage used to inform a believer's giving is 2 Corinthians 9:6-7, which says:

> *The point is this: the person who sows sparingly will also reap sparingly, and the person who sows generously will also reap generously. Each person should do as he has decided in his heart—not reluctantly or out of compulsion, since God loves a cheerful giver.*

Our giving should be voluntary and not compulsive; it should be given with gladness and not out of obligation to check-off a certain criterion. It should be given with a willing heart full of great longing for the spread of His kingdom and renown. And this principle of reaping what you sow is applicable to the whole of our lives. Galatians 6:7 says, "For whatever a person sows he will also reap." This verse is nestled in the last two chapters of Galatians where Paul instructs the believers that the Christian life is not a life in bondage to legalism. No, the Christian life is walking in the Spirit and in the costly freedom that Christ purchased on the cross. This freedom in Christ applies to every aspect of our lives!

In regard to our time and money, we are not bound to a legal system with specific marks to meet. Instead, in His deep love and good care for us, our God has given us biblical principles to guide our lives as His stewards. May we heed His truth that reminds us that we "cannot serve both God and money" (Matthew 6:24). And may we be people that are aware that a few verses prior to this hard truth is the encouragement to store up "treasures in heaven" and not on this earth. Our treasures reveal the loves of our hearts. This is why the way you spend your time and money reveals the loves of your heart. This topic has eternal value because it is an issue of the affections of our hearts.

For many of us, a large portion of our daily thoughts are on money—How will we acquire it? How will we save it? How will we spend it? It isn't wrong to have money; however, we must ensure that we have a biblical attitude toward money so that Christ remains as the supreme love of our hearts. We must not shy away from clear truths like 1 Timothy 6:10, which says, "For the love of money is a root of all kinds of evil, and by craving it, some have wandered away from the faith and pierced themselves with many griefs." Money is not inherently evil; however, it can captivate our affections and consume our desires. This can easily turn into an obsession that can drive us into a number of sins, which is why the love of money is noted as the "root of all kinds of evil." It has the potential to nurture a number of sins like greed, pride, deceit, abuse of the poor, injustice, unfaithfulness, and more.

When we don't have an affection for money, we are able to hold it loosely. We will analyze our budgets not with the intent to grow our retirement funds, but to identify areas where greater margin can be created to meet others' needs. We won't hesitate to freely give away any excess to bless others rather than engage in retail therapy simply because it's within our means. We will joyfully give as much as we're able to the church in order to invest in the spread of the kingdom of God. We will see it for what it is—a gift from God for us to steward for the glory of God. We will trust in the Giver and not the gifts to provide security. We will look to the Giver and not the gifts for true contentment and satisfaction.

This is true for all of our resources—our time, energy, talents, abilities, and more. How we choose to allocate our limited time and energy everyday will be ordered by the loves of our hearts. When we intentionally choose to help a neighbor with his overgrown yard after an exhausting workday, we are motivated by our love for Christ and His love for our neighbor. When we purposefully avoid Starbucks in order to stretch our grocery budget so that we can make dinner for a family in need or invite the pastor's family over for lunch, we are saying that we find Christ to be infinitely more satisfying than our own comforts and indulgences. Our everyday decisions are informed by our beliefs and values. May our love for Christ reign supreme, and may He reorder the loves of our hearts in such a way that it is seen in how we spend our time and money.

1. BASED ON TODAY'S PASSAGES, WHAT DOES THE WORD OF GOD SAY IN REGARD TO THE TOPIC OF GIVING TODAY?

2. CONSIDER HOW YOU SPENT YOUR TIME AND MONEY THIS PAST MONTH AND LABEL THEM YOUR TREASURES. WHAT DO YOUR TREASURES REVEAL AS THE LOVES OF YOUR HEART?

3. WE ARE FREE IN CHRIST, AND THIS FREEDOM APPLIES TO EVERY ASPECT OF OUR LIVES. HOWEVER, GOD HAS GRACIOUSLY GIVEN US BIBLICAL PRINCIPLES THAT APPLY TO HOW WE SPEND OUR TIME AND MONEY. WHAT ARE THESE PRINCIPLES? HOW DO THESE PRINCIPLES INFLUENCE HOW YOU SPEND YOUR RESOURCES?

*The filtered world of social media makes it easy
to idolize the people we follow.*

The Gospel and Social Media

READ: MATTHEW 22:36-40; PHILIPPIANS 4:8

Begin by carefully reading today's Scripture passages before coming back to this page. As you read through the passages, focus on the way that God calls us to live in relation to Him, ourselves, and others.

Social media has an influential role in all of our lives. Even if you do not personally engage in this portion of the online world, we live in a culture that is shaped by social media. There is no escaping its influence. For many of us, social media is not something we stop to think about; it is just something that we do. For others, managing the way that we use social media is a constant struggle. Whatever your level of engagement, the gospel should shape the way we view and interact with social media.

As those who have been transformed by the gospel of Jesus Christ, we are called to love God and to grow in holiness as we walk in obedience to Him. And we are called to love our neighbors as God in Christ has loved us, all for the purpose of glorifying God. Everything we do, including our use of social media, should be working toward this end, and not against it.

As children of God, we are called to love Him and doing so is the greatest commandment. Because of our sinful nature, our tendency is to love and honor and worship other things above God. This is called idolatry. One danger of social media is that it is a potential breeding ground for idolatry. The filtered world of social media makes it easy to idolize the people we follow, desiring to imitate how they look, what they do, and what they believe. They take the place of God's Word in our lives as they become our standard of what we should value, and it does not take long before we value those things more than we value God.

Social media can also expose and intensify our self-idolatry. Social media lends itself to self-centeredness where our goal is to present our best selves to the world. This kind of self-worship seeks to have others worship us as well. We may deny this desire, but the amount of time we spend trying to take the perfect picture at the perfect angle with the perfect filter and the perfect caption says otherwise. We know, literally and figuratively, how to pose to display our good side while keeping our bad side conveniently hidden away. But because of the gospel, we do not have to cover up our shortcomings and failures, because they have already been covered by the blood of Christ. We do not have to strive to live up to the standard of our social-media idols because if we are in Christ, we have His standard of righteousness as our own. We don't have to carry the weight of being our own god because we can be totally satisfied in the God who makes us look like Him.

As those who have been justified, we are called to sanctification instead of continuing to live in sin. When misused, social media can make it extremely easy to gratify the desires of the flesh rather than walk by the Spirit (Galatians 5:16). Inappropriate content is highly accessible when it comes to social media, and using social media wisely requires the self-control that comes only from the Spirit. A few taps of the finger gives us access to pornography or other sexual content that feeds our passions, but sexual content is not the only kind we should avoid. Social media can nurture all kinds of sin patterns; it can fuel envy, idolatry, and love of money. Rather than setting our hearts on what is lovely, honorable, and true, it can be a tool to fill our minds with darkness. Much of the content that is readily available to us on social media is not blatantly bad, but neither is it helpful. Whenever we engage with social media, we ought to ask ourselves: Is this edifying? Is this helping me to grow in the likeness of Christ?

Whether the content we consume on social media is positive, negative, or neutral, social media becomes a problem when it takes up excessive amounts of our time. Studies have shown that social media use releases a potentially addictive dopamine rush, and that limiting time spent on social media leads to decreased levels of anxiety and depression. It is incredibly easy to waste several hours every day on social media, even when our lives are incredibly busy. God calls us not to live our lives on autopilot, but to closely examine the things that we do and to make the best possible use of our time. When we mindlessly go to our phones, we choose not to use that time to study God's Word, meditate on Scripture, or pray. We decide not to spend that time in service to others.

The second greatest commandment is to love our neighbors, and social media can be used as a tool for or against that end. Social media has the ability to dehumanize our relationships, and we may use the relative anonymity as a reason to lash out against our neighbors in unrighteous anger. Behind the safety of our phones or computer screens, we hurl insults against those who disagree with us, saying things we would never say to someone if they were standing in front of us. This discrepancy between the way we interact with people on and offline should cause us to question ourselves: Do we love our neighbors because we have experienced the love of Christ and desire to extend that same love to others? Are we polite when we speak to someone in person because we don't want to deal with the repercussions of our rudeness? Do we really love our neighbors?

Social media is not inherently evil. We are. In our flesh, our sinful hearts take every opportunity to satisfy our sinful desires. But because of the gospel we who believe have the Holy Spirit within us empowering us to resist sin, to exercise self-control, and to walk wisely. By grace we can use social media as a powerful tool to share gospel truth. By grace social media can be a supplemental means of loving, serving, and relating to our flesh and blood neighbors. By grace God can use social media to stir our affection for Him and for His Word.

Whether it affects the way we relate to God, to ourselves, or to others, social media is not the problem. The problem is our sinful hearts. That's where the solution needs to begin.

When we are justified, we are declared to be new and righteous. However, our sinful desires still fight against the new man. This makes engaging in social media in a healthy way challenging. But the Holy Spirit sanctifies us, giving us new desires as we grow in holiness, and this process unfolds as we behold God in His Word (John 17:17, 2 Corinthians 3:18). His Word is where change happens. His glory is what transforms us.

1. WHAT DOES YOUR USE OF SOCIAL MEDIA REVEAL ABOUT THE WAY YOU RELATE TO GOD, YOURSELF, AND OTHERS? HOW DOES THE GOSPEL INFORM THESE CATEGORIES?

TO GOD:

TO YOURSELF:

TO OTHERS:

2. WHAT PRACTICAL STEPS CAN YOU TAKE TO PRACTICE SELF-CONTROL IN YOUR USE OF SOCIAL MEDIA?

3. READ JAMES 1:5, THEN WRITE A PRAYER ASKING GOD TO GIVE YOU WISDOM AS YOU NAVIGATE YOUR USE OF SOCIAL MEDIA.

Pain has a way of bringing us to a place of sweet dependence on the savior.

The Gospel for Suffering

READ: ROMANS 8:28-39, I CORINTHIANS 1:3-7, 2 CORINTHIANS 4:7-18, I PETER 1:3-9

Begin by carefully reading today's Scripture passages before coming back to this page. As you read through the passages, focus on the place of suffering in the life of the believer.

> *"I have learned to kiss the wave that throws me against the Rock of Ages."*
>
> *-Charles Spurgeon*

Do you ever become frustrated with all the big and little sufferings of life? Between the daily inconveniences and the heartbreaking tragedies, it can sometimes feel as if there are more reasons to mourn than to celebrate, and we can find ourselves despairing over the seeming meaninglessness of suffering. How can the gospel give meaning to our pain?

If this life is all there is, we will be hard pressed to find real meaning in the pain, but the good news of Jesus Christ promises an eternal hope of an inheritance that is undefiled, imperishable, and unfading (1 Peter 1:3-4). When we set our minds on the eternal promises of God, we gain new perspective on what happens in the here and now. The gospel reminds us that all of the difficulties of life, whether it be broken relationships or a broken transmission, are a result of sin and the fall, and that we can rejoice in the knowledge that every bit of our suffering is doing something magnificent in us. When Christ died on the cross, he took on our sin and condemnation and put them to death.

He rose again from the dead, declaring victory over death and ensuring our salvation. As believers, we have been united with Christ, dying with him to our sin, and being raised with him in eternal life. Because of Christ's resurrection, the good news of the gospel not only declares that the day will come when Christ will make everything right, but that every bit of suffering along the way is making us unimaginably glorious.

What does this truth mean for our everyday lives? It means that every tragedy and every inconvenience is utterly meaningful. When your car breaks down on the side of the road, God is using it to make you holy. When you lose a loved one too soon, your pain is producing beauty. When your toddler spills milk all over your freshly mopped floor, even then God is working sanctification in you. When we view life with this perspective, with our faith firmly rooted in the One who redeems and restores, our hope cannot be shaken. We may not understand exactly how God is working in our pain, but we can rest in confidence that He is transforming us into the image of Jesus Christ as He works all things together for our good (Romans 8:28-19). By the grace of God, we can begin to respond to the daily annoyances and frustrations with joy and patience, knowing that none of it is wasted.

We all know that this kind of attitude toward our pain and frustrations is not always the reality. We are quick to be angry and lash out, and our natural response to trouble is far from serene contentment and joyful patience. We are forgetful people, and we need to be reminded every day, even every moment, that God who promises to do a good work in us is faithful (Hebrews 10:23). Our need for the truth of the gospel should draw us daily to His Word, where every page points to the good news of our redemption in Him.

The gospel doesn't just offer hope for the future, but for today. God is working in our suffering in more ways than we can understand, but of one thing we can be certain—He is with us through it all. Pain has a way of bringing us to a place of sweet dependence on the savior, and God does not leave our cries unanswered. Psalm 34:18 gives the comfort that "The Lord is near the brokenhearted; He saves those crushed in spirit." In our suffering we experience the nearness of the God of all comfort in ways we could not otherwise. This is why Charles Spurgeon could learn to kiss the wave of affliction, painful though it was. God uses our deepest wounds to call us to cease from our wandering and draw near to Him.

Not only is God with us in our suffering, but Christ sympathizes with our pain (Hebrews 4:14-16). Christ is not a distant savior who snapped his fingers to save us from our sins, but a savior who humbled himself and bore the punishment for our sins, enduring all the pain and temptation that we could ever experience. When you feel as if nobody understands the pain you are going through, Jesus has felt it. When you think you are alone in your suffering, Christ is there. No matter what you go through, no matter what comes against you, you can never be separated from the love of Christ. He has compassion on you because he has endured the greatest pain, and it is in your pain that you can experience his sweet comfort. When we have suffered and felt the comforting touch of our savior, we can then comfort those who are in the midst of their own sorrows. When you experience the heartbreak of miscarriage, you can walk alongside other parents facing the same loss. When you have walked through uncertainty when you lose a job, you can tell your friend who has been laid off of the faithfulness of God in your life to supply every need. When you have been given a song in your darkest night, you can sing it over those in the midst of darkness.

When we view our pain in light of the resurrection, there is indescribable hope. Because Christ is risen, your suffering, like His, will result in glory. Because Christ is risen, we have a living hope of an eternal inheritance that nothing can touch. Because Christ is risen, our living savior is with us to comfort, to empower, and to guide. Christ's resurrection ensures that we, too, will be resurrected in glorified bodies that will be free from all pain, and that our savior who suffered for us will wipe every tear from our eyes.

1. HOW DOES THE RESURRECTION GIVE US PERSPECTIVE AND HOPE IN OUR PAIN?

2. WHAT REPEATED WORD(S) DO YOU SEE IN I CORINTHIANS 1:3-7? WHAT DOES THIS REPETITION REVEAL ABOUT GOD'S CHARACTER AND OUR SUFFERING?

3. WHEN WE EXPERIENCE SUFFERING, WE NEED TO REMEMBER HOW GOD HAS BEEN FAITHFUL IN THE PAST. GIVE AN EXAMPLE FROM YOUR OWN LIFE, ANOTHER BELIEVER'S LIFE, OR SCRIPTURE OF HOW GOD HAS BEEN FAITHFUL IN THE MIDST OF SUFFERING.

*The answer is the gospel and preaching
the gospel to yourself every day.*

Preaching the Gospel to Yourself

READ: ROMANS 3:19-26, GALATIANS 5:16-26, EPHESIANS 6:10-17, PSALM 42

Begin by carefully reading today's Scripture passages. As you read through the passages, remind yourself of the beauty of the gospel that you heard when you first believed. Then consider how your true identity in Christ has implications for how you live every day.

When tragedy strikes or we find ourselves in a moment of crisis, we may naturally find ourselves running to God in prayer and in His Word. Our lives on this side of eternity will inevitably be marked by times of pain and suffering because of sin and our unredeemed flesh. However, for the majority of us, the bulk of our days will be ordinary. We'll be busy at our day jobs to pay the bills. We'll wipe runny noses, mop sticky floors, and spend hours in the car taking our kids to their after-school activities. However, the truth remains: whether we are in a season of suffering or comfort, we need the gospel. And we need the gospel every single day because we are sinners — we may be sinners saved by grace alone through faith alone in Christ alone, but we are still sinners. We still wrestle with unbelief and our flesh on a daily basis until Christ returns.

Believers should aim to saturate every moment of every day with gospel truth. Rather than relying on gospel catchphrases in moments of crisis, it should be a language that is utilized and laced throughout our ordinary days. As believers, we have heard the gospel because, by His grace, we have responded by putting our faith in Christ and have been redeemed. We are not naturally inclined to suddenly see our lives in light of the work and person of Christ. We need to grow in our understanding of the gospel in order to have it inform our thoughts, feelings, and perceptions. So a good place to start is the gospel. What is it? And how exactly does the person and work of Christ apply to the ordinary moments of our days?

A helpful verse that succinctly encapsulates the good news is 2 Corinthians 5:21, which says, "He made the one who did not know sin to be sin for us, so that in Him we might become the righteousness of God." Jesus, the sinless Son of God, willingly took on flesh and became fully man. God the Father, in His grand plan of redemption, treated His Son as if He were a sinner, and sent Him to die as a substitute to pay the penalty of death for the sins of those who would believe in Him. Jesus satisfied the wrath of God on the cross. Furthermore, He gives His righteousness, His own perfect record, to those very sinners! This is the gospel — we are justified and have positional holiness in Christ. However, the gospel also brings about our sanctification. We bear His righteousness, but we are also being made righteous, which is our sanctification. And this is a lifelong pursuit — yes, the Holy

Spirit is the One who sanctifies us, but we also partner with Him by gazing at the glory of Christ. This is how we are transformed into Christlikeness, which is the ultimate goal of every believer, and this is why the gospel applies to us every single day. It is a progressive sanctification as we are transformed from "one degree of glory to another" (2 Corinthians 3:18).

Every day, we engage in battle. There is a war between our flesh and the Spirit. Our flesh is every sinful inclination of our human, fallen nature. For some of us, our workplaces are filled with opportunities to sin in the form of unwholesome talk, gossip, slander, lust, idleness, grumbling, deceit, and covetousness. For others, our days are filled with the demands of taking care of a newborn and a toddler or two. We may wrestle with unrighteous anger when our preferences are not met by our children or we're plagued with anxiety— over the bills, our health, our family's safety, and our futures. The battle can be more insidious for others—maybe we're in full-time ministry and we're wrestling with self-righteousness and pride. Our battles may look different because our minds, emotions, and life circumstances are different. Regardless of our differences, our unredeemed humanness points us to the common need for the gospel every day. But instead, many of us attempt to remedy our restlessness by escaping into the false reality of social media, or we quiet our thoughts and feelings by numbing ourselves with Netflix or other forms of mindless entertainment. Or we look into ourselves—we resolve to work harder at our jobs and homes, as if our wills can quiet the nagging accusation that we're not enough.

Is there a better way? Yes, and the answer is the gospel and preaching the gospel to yourself every day. The good news of saving grace that led to your saving faith is the good news of sanctifying grace that grows your faith. Whenever we are faced with sin, we apply the gospel by asking ourselves some basic questions: Who is God? What has He done? Who am I in light of who He is and what He has done? How should my identity in Him impact the way that I respond to this situation? In the midst of the everyday battle against sin, we answer these questions, and in so doing, we preach the gospel to ourselves.

So when we are plagued with anxiety, we can apply the gospel by reminding ourselves who our God is—He is good, all-powerful, and trustworthy. And we know this to be true because of what He has done. He willingly took on flesh and died on the cross for us while we were His enemies. He conquered the grave and is now at the right hand of God the Father! And when we put our faith in Him, we are His child and our identity is in Christ. The implications of being in Christ are widespread, and we find them in His Word. So as believers, we need to know the Word of God. We put on the armor of God and wield the sword of the Spirit, which is the Word of God as we go into battle (Ephesians 6:17). Often this battle is in our minds. It is then that we stop our wandering thoughts and "take every thought captive to obey Christ" (2 Corinthians 10:5). We capture the thought and bring it under the Word to see if it is true. If it is not, we replace it with truth from Scripture. This is what the author of Psalm 42 does in his state of depression—he tells himself to, "Put your hope in God." As we strive to apply the gospel to every aspect of our lives, may we remember to preach the gospel to ourselves everyday.

1. WHAT IS THE GOSPEL? HOW IS YOUR GOSPEL FLUENCY?

2. CONSIDER YOUR LIFE. WHAT PARTICULAR SIN PATTERNS DO YOU SEE IN YOUR LIFE? HOW CAN ANSWERING THE QUESTIONS ABOUT WHO GOD IS, WHAT HE HAS DONE, AND WHO YOU ARE IN LIGHT OF THOSE TRUTHS HELP YOU OVERCOME THOSE SINS?

3. WHAT IS ONE THING YOU CAN DO TO REMIND YOURSELF OF THE GOSPEL EVERY SINGLE DAY?

"

Why are you cast down, O my soul, and why are you in turmoil within me? Hope in God; for I shall again praise him, my salvation and my God.

PSALM 42:11

PARAPHRASE THE PASSAGES FROM THIS WEEK.

_____
_____
_____
_____
_____
_____
_____
_____
_____

WHAT DID YOU OBSERVE FROM THIS WEEK'S TEXT ABOUT
GOD AND HIS CHARACTER?

_____
_____
_____
_____
_____

WHAT DO THESE PASSAGES TEACH ABOUT THE CONDITION OF
MANKIND AND ABOUT YOURSELF?

_____
_____
_____
_____
_____
_____
_____

HOW DO THESE PASSAGES POINT TO THE GOSPEL?

HOW SHOULD YOU RESPOND TO THESE PASSAGES?
WHAT IS THE PERSONAL APPLICATION?

WHAT SPECIFIC ACTION STEPS CAN YOU TAKE THIS WEEK
TO APPLY THESE PASSAGES?

READ. PRAY. MEDITATE. MEMORIZE.
Preach the Gospel to Yourself.

IN ALL CIRCUMSTANCES

1 Corinthians 10:31
2 Corinthians 5:21
Philippians 4:11-13

IN CONDEMNATION & SHAME

Romans 8:1
Titus 3:4-6

IN DECISION MAKING

James 1:5
Psalm 37:23-24

FOR SPIRITUAL DISCIPLINES

Psalm 119:18
1 Thessalonians 5:16-18

WHEN YOU ARE OVERWHELMED

Psalm 42:11
Matthew 11:28-30
2 Corinthians 12:9

FOR PHYSICAL HEALTH

1 Timothy 4:7-8
1 Corinthians 6:19-20

IN MARRIAGE

Matthew 19:6
Colossians 3:18-19

IN SINGLENESS

Revelation 19:6-8
Isaiah 56:1-7

IN PARENTING

Deuteronomy 6:4-7
Philippians 4:6-7

IN DISCIPLESHIP

Matthew 28:19-20
Hebrews 3:13

IN SEASONS OF WAITING

Psalm 27:13-14
Isaiah 64:4

FOR HOSPITALITY

1 Peter 4:8-9
Hebrews 13:2

THE LOCAL CHURCH

Hebrews 10:25
Romans 12:3-8

IN COMMUNITY

John 13:34-35
Ephesians 4:25-32

IN FRIENDSHIP

Romans 12:10
Proverbs 27:6

IN WORK

Colossians 3:23
Acts 20:35

IN FREE TIME

Ephesians 5:15-17
1 Corinthians 10:31

IN RESOURCES

2 Corinthians 9:6-7
Luke 12:32-34

FOR SOCIAL MEDIA

Galatians 5:16
Hebrews 10:24

IN SUFFERING

1 Peter 5:10
2 Corinthians 4:7-18

Preaching the Gospel to Yourself in Prayer

A helpful exercise to develop this habit of preaching the gospel to yourself is starting your day with gospel truths. The prayer below is offered to get you started.

Father,

Thank You that You are God and I am not. I confess that I am a sinner—in words, thoughts, deeds, and motives. I fall short and sin every day. Thank You that I can run to Jesus through faith and be confident that His work on the cross fully satisfies the wrath of God. I know my sins are forgiven! And not only that, but I am declared righteous before the Father! I have been given the righteousness of Christ. Thank You, Jesus, that You are my righteousness! You lived a life of perfect obedience that I could never live. Thank You for Your steadfast love towards me. I am Your beloved. Though I still wrestle with my flesh, I am a saint because of my union with Christ. You are mighty and powerful. Jesus, You conquered the grave in Your resurrection, and Your Word says that I am more than a conqueror. Thank You that Your Spirit lives in me. I am not alone, and He empowers me to overcome sin in my life. Holy Spirit, convict me when my thoughts and feelings go astray from these gospel truths. Thank You that You are for me. You have orchestrated all things in my life to bring about holiness. I can trust in You. Help me to love You with all of my heart, soul, mind, and strength, and help me to love my neighbors as myself. May I lean on Your grace today to live for the praise of Your glory.

In Jesus' name I pray,
Amen

True Identity in Christ

Who are you? If you are a believer, your identity is in Christ. You don't have to look to the temporary things of this world for your identity; you can rest in Christ who has established your true identity through His death and resurrection.

IN CHRIST, YOU ARE:	IN SIN, YOU ARE:
Justified by His grace (Romans 3:24)	Wicked with evil intentions (Genesis 6:5)
Dead to sin and alive to God (Romans 6:11)	Separated from God (Isaiah 59:2)
No longer condemned (Romans 8:1)	Unclean and polluted (Isaiah 64:6)
Free from the law of sin and death (Romans 8:2)	Condemned (Romans 8:1)
Member of the body of Christ (Romans 12:5)	A slave to sin (Romans 6:20)
Wise (1 Corinthians 4:10)	Dead in your trespasses and sins (Ephesians 2:1)
Washed and sanctified (1 Corinthians 6:11)	Son of disobedience (Ephesians 2:2)
Hopeful (1 Corinthians 15:19)	In bondage to Satan (Ephesians 2:2)
A new creation (2 Corinthians 5:19)	Children of wrath (Ephesians 2:3)
A son of God (Galatians 3:26)	Recipient of God's wrath (Romans 2:5)
Recipient of every spiritual blessing (Ephesians 1:3)	Fall short of the glory of God (Romans 3:23)
Alive (Ephesians 2:5)	Enemy of God (Romans 5:10)
His workmanship created for good works (Ephesians 2:10)	Blind to Truth (2 Corinthians 4:4)
Partaker of the promise (Ephesians 3:6)	Deceived (2 Corinthians 11:3)
Forgiven (Ephesians 4:32)	Guilty of breaking the law (James 2:2)
Saint (Philippians 4:21)	
Saved (2 Timothy 1:9)	
Called to a holy calling (2 Timothy 1:9)	
Strengthened by grace (2 Timothy 2:10)	

WHAT IS *the Gospel?*

Thank you for reading and enjoying this study with us! We are abundantly grateful for the Word of God, the instruction we glean from it, and the ever-growing understanding about God's character from it. We're also thankful that Scripture continually points to one thing in innumerable ways: the gospel.

We remember our brokenness when we read about the fall of Adam and Eve in the garden of Eden (Genesis 3), when sin entered into a perfect world and maimed it. We remember the necessity that something innocent must die to pay for our sin when we read about the atoning sacrifices in the Old Testament. We read that we have all sinned and fallen short of the glory of God (Romans 3:23), and that the penalty for our brokenness, the wages of our sin, is death (Romans 6:23). We all are in need of grace, mercy, and most importantly: we all need a Savior.

We consider the goodness of God when we realize that He did not plan to leave us in this dire state. We see His promise to buy us back from the clutches of sin and death in Genesis 3:15. And we see that promise accomplished with Jesus Christ on the cross. Jesus Christ knew no sin yet became sin so that we might become righteous through His sacrifice (2 Corinthians 5:21). Jesus was tempted in every way that we are and lived sinlessly. He was reviled, yet still yielded Himself for our sake, that we may have life abundant in Him. Jesus lived the perfect life that we could not live, and died the death that we deserved.

The gospel is profound yet simple. There are many mysteries in it that we can never exhaust this side of heaven, but there is still overwhelming weight to its implications in this life. The gospel is the telling of our sinfulness and God's goodness, and this gracious gift compels a response. We are saved by grace through faith, which means that we rest with faith in the grace that Jesus Christ displayed on the cross (Ephesians 2:9). We cannot save ourselves from our brokenness or do any amount of good works to merit God's favor, but we can have faith that what Jesus accomplished in His death, burial, and resurrection was more than enough for our salvation and our eternal delight. When we accept God, we are commanded to die to our self and our sinful desires, and live a life worthy of the calling we've received (Ephesians 4:1). The gospel compels us to be sanctified, and in so doing, we are conformed to the likeness of Christ Himself.

This is hope. This is redemption. This is the gospel.

Thank You

FOR STUDYING GOD'S
WORD WITH US!

CONNECT WITH US:

@THEDAILYGRACECO
@KRISTINSCHMUCKER

CONTACT US:

INFO@THEDAILYGRACECO.COM

SHARE:

#THEDAILYGRACECO
#LAMPANDLIGHT

WEBSITE:

WWW.THEDAILYGRACECO.COM

———